WISDOM

from

MYLES
MUNROE

BOOKS BY MYLES MUNROE

Applying the Kingdom

God's Big Idea

In Pursuit of Purpose

Kingdom Parenting

Kingdom Principles

Myles Munroe 365-Day Devotional

Overcoming Crisis

Rediscovering Faith

Rediscovering the Kingdom

Releasing Your Potential

Single, Married, Separated and Life After Divorce

The Glory of Living

The Purpose and Power of Love & Marriage

The Purpose and Power of Praise & Worship

Understanding Your Potential

Waiting and Dating

Wisdom from Myles Munroe

AVAILABLE FROM DESTINY IMAGE PUBLISHERS

WISDOM

from

MYLES

MUNROE

Myles Munroe

DESTINY IMAGE® PUBLISHERS, INC.

P.O. Box 310, Shippensburg, PA 17257-0310

"Speaking to the Purposes of God for This Generation and for the Generations to Come."

This book and all other Destiny Image, Revival Press, MercyPlace, Fresh Bread, Destiny Image Fiction, and Treasure House books are available at Christian bookstores and distributors worldwide.

For a U.S. bookstore nearest you, call **1-800-722-6774.**

For more information on foreign distributors, call **717-532-3040.**

Reach us on the Internet: **www.destinyimage.com.**

Trade Paper ISBN 13: 978-0-7684-3288-6

Hardcover ISBN 13: 978-0-7684-3228-2

Large Print ISBN 13: 978-0-7684-3411-8

Ebook ISBN 13: 978-0-7684-9068-8

For Worldwide Distribution, Printed in the U.S.A.

3 4 5 6 7 8 9 10 11 / 23 22 21

Contents

Introduction

Solomon asked God for it. Universities espouse its virtues. Pastors pray for it. Parents want to believe their children have it. Students hope for it. Executives bank on it. Some rationalize it. Others brag about it. Most want more of it.

Within today's 24-7 communication culture, it is many times hard to recognize truth from fiction, wisdom from folly. In our virtual reality worldwide society, someone's "wisdom" can be—and is—blogged, Twittered, Skyped, emailed, and Facebooked instantaneously to others next door or in a faraway continent. Allowing wisdom to become relative is opening doors for imposters to barge in. Only with God's wisdom can believers forge ahead to make the world a safer, stronger, and more beautiful place.

How much better to get wisdom than gold! And to get understanding is to be chosen rather than silver (Proverbs 16:16 NKJV).

God's wisdom, shared through His committed and dedicated servants, has carried people through ages past full of danger, through current economic and worldwide unrest, and will continue to protect and defend His children throughout eternity. Only wisdom from Heaven provides peace that passes all human understanding.

Wisdom From Myles Munroe is a compilation of bits of wisdom received from the Lord over many years of serving Him. Shared with you are 40 wise and personal insights to refresh and empower you to tackle life's challenges, rejoice in God's promises fulfilled, and shout victory over the enemy.

This interactive devotional journal immerses you into a world where God's powerful wisdom infuses you as never before. You will gain the strength to solve problems, turn situations around, and learn how to make wise decisions.

Within each chapter are wise reflections from best-selling books along with provocative "Points to Ponder" that help you delve into the depths of yourself to search out things, issues, people, situations, and just plain stuff that you need to deal with to be able to move forward toward your God-given destiny.

"Words of Wisdom" from other well-known believers will make you laugh, cry, and become a more thinking Christian as you consider other points of view about important topics. A place for your own special thoughts is provided to record your heart's desires, feelings, ideas, wonderings, and inner yearnings.

This treasured keepsake launches you onto a road filled with wisdom and paved with God's glory.

1

Wisdom for Everyday Victory

What do you do when everything you trusted in collapses? How do you prepare for a sudden change in life? How do you recover when life hits you on your blind side? After a lifetime of hard work, dedication, commitment, and loyalty to a chosen career, how do you suddenly change your vocation and skill sets? What do you do when a lifelong dream and investment is suddenly taken from you through no fault of your own? How do you bounce back after institutions that were expected to protect you suddenly pull the rug out from under your life? What do you say to your family when you face the reality that you may no longer be able to fulfill their expectations for security, support, and provision?

(Excerpts from *Overcoming Crisis*)

Wisdom Reflections

WHERE do you go when you want to work, but there are no jobs? What do you do when your sense of pride for personal accomplishment is dashed in the fires of survival? How do you go on after the legacy of years of work is erased by a pink slip from the company you helped build? How do you face the family you once left to find your fortune and chase your dreams and ask them to take you back in because your world has evaporated? Where do you go when the ones you go to for help are also in need of help?

Living on earth requires that we must expect the unexpected and prepare for the unforeseen. It's the nature of life. But many of us do not possess the necessary mental, emotional, psychological, and spiritual tools to successfully and effectively weather these seasons of turmoil.

You must understand that *the Kingdom of God is never in crisis*. Let that sink in. The Kingdom is never in crisis mode because the King is bigger than any crisis that has ever happened, will ever happen, or is happening right now. He knows what to do.

Not only does He know what to do, but also He cares for us, both individually and corporately. He loves people. And God has never failed His people yet. The important thing is to make sure that you are one of His people.

This book of wisdom is about how to make sure that you are walking according to His principles as a citizen of His

Kingdom. It will help you hold up a measuring rod to your current situation, and it will show you how to measure up to His righteous standards so that you, too, can overcome every crisis. Then you can turn to help your neighbor on the way. If you claim citizenship in the Kingdom of Heaven, you have a way out of every crisis.

Notice that I did not promise you a crisis-free life. No, I promise you a way out, a way to overcome each crisis, whether big or small. Nobody is exempt from crises, including Christians. You *will* have crises. Jesus said, *"...In this world you will have trouble. But take heart! I have overcome the world"* (John 16:33).

Points to Ponder

Are you expecting the unexpected
and preparing for the unforeseen?

Do you possess the necessary mental, emotional,
psychological, and spiritual tools to successfully
and effectively weather seasons of turmoil?

Always remember: the Kingdom of God is never in crisis.

God knows what to do—He cares for you.

God has never failed His people.

Are you sure that you are one of His people?

Words of Wisdom

Regardless of the family you were born into, or the circumstances surrounding your birth, God had foreknowledge of your arrival long before your conception. There's victory in knowing that your birth was not accidental, and that you have a specific purpose to fulfill during your lifetime.

—Joseph W. Walker III, *Life Between Sundays*[1]

Lord, You are the God of peace and harmony, You will soon crush satan under Your feet; May the grace of the Lord Jesus Christ rest on me.

—Elmer L. Towns, *Praying Paul's Letters*[2]

For the most part, we've had a theologically informed worldview that has seamlessly matched reality. But God has called us to that place of heavenly perspective, the Glory realm, and the reality of the supernatural in our daily lives. It's a radical shift from an earthly perspective to a heavenly one.

As God's children, *imago deo,* made in His image and likeness as spiritual beings, we have similar faculties of mind, will, and emotion to the Father. Like begets like, so in truth, each one of us has the potential to walk, live, and have our being in the supernatural ways of God in order to fulfill our mission and very purpose for being here.

—Jeff Jansen, *Glory Rising*[3]

Assurance is the fruit that grows out of the root of faith.

—Stephen Charnock

13

MY WISDOM KEYS

_____

_____

_____

_____

_____

_____

_____

_____

_____

_____

_____

_____

_____

2

Wisdom During Crisis

What constitutes a "crisis"? How bad does a situation have to be? What kind of crises have you been through in your life? What kind of crisis are you in right now?

It is true that what can seem like a crisis to one person is not a crisis to someone else. Yet for everyone, a crisis is an event over which one has no control. Crises are experiences that you did not anticipate or prepare for. They take you by surprise, and they fill you with anxiety.

(Excerpts from *Overcoming Crisis*)

Wisdom Reflections

LET'S say the weather forecast says that a hurricane is coming. Here in the Bahamas, we know that could be serious. We know that when hurricanes hit, they don't mess around. Suddenly your priorities are different. If you were planning to go visit your friend, you change your plan. If you have a family, you try to make sure they will be safe. You do whatever you have to do to get ready for the storm before it hits your neighborhood.

Or say the doctor says, "You've got three weeks to live if you don't change your habits." He is not joking. All of a sudden, you get motivated to change. This is a crisis. You may not be able to avoid all of the consequences of your eating habits, your smoking, or whatever, but you will probably clean up your act. You will stop eating cheesecake and macaroni salad on the same plate, and you will start eating raw carrots. You may have been trying to stop smoking for 50 years without success, but now, instantly, you will stop cold turkey.

A crisis forces the issue. You cannot control the crisis that has come upon you, but you can begin to control some of the details of your predicament. You can make some headway against it. Later on, you may even be able to appreciate the crisis for forcing you to change. (One thing I *like* about hurricanes is that they clean things up. All the rotten trees, the poor construction, the junk lying around—the hurricane comes through and creates a mess. But five months later, the mess has been cleaned up and you see a cleaned-up landscape, new flowers, new buildings.)

Jesus said that we will always have troubles (see John 16:33). One crisis after another will come our way as long as we live, regardless of how well-insulated we try to make ourselves. So it is important to get a grip on how to overcome not only some of the circumstances, but also—especially—our emotional responses to difficulties. If we can regain our emotional footing in a storm, we will be able to overcome. First, before we can regain our emotional footing, we need to put our feet on the Rock-solid foundation of God.

Points to Ponder

What crisis are you facing today?

Are you facing your crisis alone or with God?

You cannot control the crisis that has come upon you suddenly, but you can take control of some of the details.

Get a grip on how to overcome your circumstances.

Regain your emotional footing to overcome a crisis.

Put your feet on the Rock-solid foundation of God.

Words of Wisdom

A righteous man may have many troubles, but the Lord delivers him from them all (Psalm 34:19).

౿

To be sure, the future was wrought with difficulty, trouble, mistakes, but I knew that He was the God of great patience, mercy, and forgiveness. As often as I messed up, He would forgive me and urge me forward. I knew it. I experienced it. He gave me strength and I was beginning to hear Him speak to me and restore my soul.

—Don Nori Sr., *You Can Pray in Tongues*[1]

౿

You will have no test of faith that will not fit you to be a blessing if you are obedient to the Lord. I never had a trial but when I got out of the deep river I found some poor pilgrim on the bank that I was able to help by that very experience.

—A.B. Simpson

౿

Praying for the poor, the brokenhearted, and the prisoners of darkness will not compromise our intimacy with our heavenly Father. Rather, God draws close to those who pray to be sent to the front lines to advance His purposes.

—Joseph Mattera, *Kingdom Revolution*[2]

MY WISDOM KEYS

_____

_____

_____

_____

_____

_____

_____

_____

_____

_____

_____

_____

3

Wisdom Versus Greed

Greed walks hand-in-hand with partners such as malice, deceit, theft, envy, evil thoughts, lewdness, adultery, slander, arrogance, murder, and all kinds of folly (see Mark 7:21-22). The reason these evils travel together is because all of them originate in the sinful hearts of human beings. In many ways, they represent aspects of greed. Theft is greed for things that are perceived as valuable to the thief. Envy and slander represent a greed for reputation. Lewdness and adultery are forms of sexual greed. Arrogance and murder amount to greed for power and vengeance.

(Excerpts from *Overcoming Crisis*)

Wisdom Reflections

"ALL RIGHT," you might say, "so we can blame the economic mess on the greed of the fat cats in high places. What good does that do me as I stand in the unemployment line?"

For one thing, it can be a caution to you. Do not take the same path yourself. Do not let your own financial uncertainty make you do something rash and foolish. Do not do something dishonest. Do not go the way of the world. Do not worry about yourself. Instead, put your trust in God and ask Him what to do. He knows what to tell you. He's just waiting for you to stop trying to solve things yourself and to start to pay attention to His directions.

If you pay attention, you will know when He is pricking your conscience. He will warn you when your heart starts to brew up some form of malice, deceit, theft, envy, evil thoughts, lewdness, adultery, slander, arrogance, murder, or other kinds of folly.

When Jesus said "watch out," He meant that it could happen to you, especially if you do not even know you're greedy. Here you are, driving to work in your used car. You pass someone's shiny new car. You do not need a new car. Your old car is working fine, and it is paid for. What are you going to say?—"Oh, the Lord is gonna bless me with a new car." What makes you think that would be a blessing? You don't need any new car. If you get one, you're going to have to go into debt. You call that a blessing? God calls it a debt. The car you already have is good enough. Next time you go somewhere in it, take Jesus' advice: "Watch out! Be on your guard against all kinds of greed; a man's life does not consist in the abundance of his possessions."

I will never forget the day I went to visit the late John Templeton. He greeted me with a smile, and he kissed me. In front of me I saw this old man in worn-out shorts and tennis shoes with holes. Mr. Templeton of the Templeton Foundation, worth billions of dollars, gave me a tour through his little office.

This man was giving away more than a million dollars every year to people who had contributed something exceptional to the world's understanding of God. He had his priorities straight. He was so wealthy partly because he gave away so much.

Points to Ponder

Evils travel together because all of them
originate in the sinful hearts of human beings.

Do not let your financial uncertainty make
you do something rash and foolish.

Do not do something dishonest.

Do not go the way of the world.

Do not worry about yourself.

Put your trust in God and ask Him what to do.

Words of Wisdom

If our goods are not available to the community, they are stolen goods.

—Martin Luther

⌒

"You didn't get the job, Sid. Tough, man. The Port Authority representative said you acted like you thought the world owed you a living. He said you'd probably have two or three jobs before you'd realize the world doesn't revolve around you."

—from *There Must be Something More* by Sid Roth[1]

⌒

A greedy man stirs up dissension, but he who trusts in the Lord will prosper (Proverbs 28:25).

⌒

The person who refuses to compromise under any and every circumstance is obstinate, unreasonable, and selfish. That sort of strong-willed inflexibility is sinful and has been the ruin of many relationships and organizations. But when it comes to matters of principle—moral and ethical foundations, biblical absolutes, the axioms of God's Word, God's clear commands, and the truthfulness of God Himself—it is never right to compromise.

—John MacArthur, *The Book on Leadership*[2]

⌒

Be shepherds of God's flock that is under your care, serving as overseers— not because you must, but because you are willing, as God wants you to be; not greedy for money, but eager to serve (1 Peter 5:2).

4

Wisdom and Opportunity

You will often hear it said that the words for *crisis* in Japanese and Chinese are the same as the word *opportunity*. There's wonderful truth in that. You wouldn't think that those two words have anything in common until you realize that the seeming defeat inherent in every crisis holds the keys to an unanticipated victory. When the atomic bomb was dropped on Hiroshima at the end of World War II, it obliterated the city. Over a hundred thousand people are estimated to have been killed. The buildings were leveled. The soil was poisoned. But the Japanese people took hold of the hands that reached out to help them, and they worked day and night to rebuild their city and their country. You know what happened. Now they are number one in so many categories: their cars, their electronics, and a lot more.

(Excerpts from *Overcoming Crisis*)

Wisdom Reflections

YOU see, if you think this way, every disaster gets turned in a new direction. Your crisis becomes your best opportunity. If your house burns down, you don't despair. Instead, as soon as you can, you seize this opportunity to build a new and better house. If you get laid off from your job, you either find a better one, or you create a better one by going into business for yourself. Out of your crisis comes your opportunity.

If you call it an *opportunity* instead of buckling under the load of the words *crisis* or *tragedy* or *disaster,* then you can start taking advantage of what has happened. You stop thinking of yourself as somebody who lost a job and start thinking of this as the first time you have been set free from a job. Now you can do something new!

The rest of the world will continue to wallow in all those results of a crisis: fear, trauma, depression, despair, frustration, anxiety, loneliness, worry, hopelessness, a sense of abandonment, a sense of loss, a sense of death, an urgency for survival, abuse, crime, domestic violence, and substance abuse.

But not you, because you are not under the world's system. You will rub shoulders all the time with people who are anxious and afraid. You will hear people express how lonely they feel, how they feel as if they are the only ones having such big problems. They will get more and more desperate, while you and everyone else who does it God's way will be busy stepping up on top of your problems to get a better view. Once you really step up on them, you can see much farther than you could see before. The air is better up there.

Instead of worrying, rejoice. *"Rejoice in the Lord always. Again I will say, rejoice!"* (Phil. 4:4 NKJV). Do not throw away your confidence. He who began a good work in you will finish it. (See Philippians 1:6.) You do not have to wait for Heaven. What you are going through right now is only a test. And, I promise you, there is an abundance of life after the test, right here on earth.

Points to Ponder

The seeming defeat inherent in every crisis
holds the keys to an unanticipated victory.

Believe that your crisis becomes your best opportunity.

Remember, you are not under the world's system.

Instead of worrying, rejoice.

Do not throw away your confidence.

God, who began a good work in you, will finish it.

Words of Wisdom

Be very careful, then, how you live—not as unwise but as wise, making the most of every opportunity, because the days are evil. Therefore do not be foolish, but understand what the Lord's will is (Ephesians 5:15-17).

All of us experience times of crisis. This is an opportune time for the small group or house church to get actively involved in practical ministry. ...When a storm brought a huge tree crashing down on their house roof, one family experienced God's love in action through their small group. "Love started flowing our way the very next day...."

—Larry Kreider, *House to House*[1]

I was seldom able to see an opportunity until it had ceased to be one.

—Mark Twain

Opportunity is missed by most people because it is dressed in overalls and looks like work.

—Thomas Edison

Therefore, as we have opportunity, let us do good to all people, especially to those who belong to the family of believers (Galatians 6:10).

MY WISDOM KEYS

_____

_____

_____

_____

_____

_____

_____

_____

_____

_____

_____

_____

5

Wisdom of Management

The culture of Heaven is a culture of plenty—but only if it gets managed right. It is true that God created human beings to worship Him, but He already had plenty of worshipers in Heaven, so He did not create humans in order to obtain more worship. Heaven has always been packed full of worshipers. When God turned His attention to filling the earth with good things, He decided to create people in His own image to manage the earth.

(Excerpts from *Overcoming Crisis*)

Wisdom Reflections

BECAUSE God made us managers from the beginning, when He created Adam and Eve and placed them in the Garden of Eden, management (sometimes called *stewardship*) is a primary goal of the human race, whether people realize it or not. When we follow the Master Plan, we flourish. And, like Adam and Eve, when we mismanage, we lose. Although it has no effect on the management mandate of God whether we manage well or poorly, it does have an effect on how much of His Kingdom can express itself on earth.

Let's bring it home: when you keep coming to work late, you can lose your job. When you keep eating too much fat, you can lose your health. When you do not cultivate your friendships, they can die. If you do not keep on putting affection and respect into your marriage, it falls apart. Whatever you mismanage, you start losing. Whatever you manage properly, you protect.

Proper management is the *correct use* of something. To use something correctly implies that you will use it with integrity. You will not slip into dishonesty. If you are not supposed to use the copier at work, you will not make personal copies on it. You won't even help yourself to a paper clip. That paper clip wasn't given to you for your private use. It is somebody else's property. I know it's very small and that your boss won't miss it, but if you are managing your work properly, you will not take it home. Once you put it in your pocket without a twinge of conscience, then it is easier to graduate from a paper clip to a pencil to a stapler to a laptop computer. The principle is honesty, and that is more important than a paper clip.

Proper management is *timely use* of another person's property. (And remember that even your own property doesn't wholly belong to you.) That means you get your timing right. When the country has been plunged into economic uncertainty, you postpone remodeling your house. You change your vacation plans—unless you already live in Hawaii, you don't buy your ticket to Maui yet. You pull back. You reassess. You reorganize. You figure out what your resources are, and then you proceed to use them wisely, timing your use of them based on what you can observe and on what the Spirit of God prompts you to do.

Points to Ponder

God created people in His own image to manage the earth.

When you follow the Master Plan, you will flourish.

When you mismanage, you lose.

The principle is honesty.

Proper management is timely use
of another person's property.

Figure out what your resources are,
and then use them wisely.

Words of Wisdom

Jesus told His disciples: "There was a rich man whose manager was accused of wasting his possessions. So he called him in and asked him, 'What is this I hear about you? Give an account of your management, because you cannot be manager any longer.'" The manager said to himself, "What shall I do now? My master is taking away my job. I'm not strong enough to dig, and I'm ashamed to beg (Luke 16:1-3).

∽

And I'd say one of the great lessons I've learned over the past couple of decades, from a management perspective, is that really when you come down to it, it really is all about people and all about leadership.

—Steve Case, former CEO of AOL

∽

Unity speaks of proper alignment, and oil speaks of the anointing of the Holy Spirit—of grace. When I aligned myself under spiritual authority, a level of grace began to flow in my life that I had never before experienced, because the oil that was flowing from the head started to run all over me.

—Banning Leibscher, *Jesus Culture*[1]

∽

Management is efficiency in climbing the ladder of success; leadership determines whether the ladder is leaning against the right wall.

—Stephen R. Covey, *The 7 Habits of Highly Effective People*

MY WISDOM KEYS

_____

_____

_____

_____

_____

_____

_____

_____

_____

_____

_____

_____

_____

_____

6

Wisdom and Faith

We live in a consumer-driven culture, and it is in a crisis all the time. The society around us is obsessed with *things*. People are perpetually tired and worn out, distracted and depressed, irritable and in a hurry. They suffer from stress-induced illnesses, and they treat each other poorly.

The Kingdom of God is not like that in the least. The resources we need are supposed to come to us in the natural course of living our lives according to God's design and intention. We do not seek the Kingdom of God because of its benefits, but its benefits come to us as we seek the Kingdom. The provisions and resources that we need are not meant to become the objects of our faith. They are meant to be the by-products of our faith.

(Excerpts from *Overcoming Crisis*)

Wisdom Reflections

KINGDOM-DWELLERS have faith. Their faith grows as they exercise it daily. True Kingdom people do not treat their faith as a tool or a trick. When they exercise their faith, it is not like playing a slot machine, where if they somehow end up with the right combination of words and actions, they win.

Rather, it is a relationship, albeit with an invisible King. This King of ours has communicated liberally with His people, especially through His written Word. He has displayed his laws and His principles and has made them accessible to all who have eyes to see and ears to hear.

God's Son, Jesus, came to preach the Kingdom of God. He did not confuse His listeners when He said, *"Seek first the kingdom of God and His righteousness, and all these things shall be added to you"* (Matt. 6:33 NKJV). For a member of the family of the Kingdom, what was truly worth seeking? Only two things: the Kingdom itself and the righteousness that comes from God.

A Kingdom person does not live for a job. A Kingdom person does not live for a spouse. A Kingdom person does not live to gather blessings. Rather a Kingdom person lives to display the love of God to the society around him or her. A Kingdom person may revert to old habits of self-protection, but soon remembers that God wants to supply every need.

The King is both Father and Savior. He is omnipotent, which means "all-powerful." He is omniscient, which means "all-knowing." He is omnipresent, which means He is everywhere at the same time. Therefore, we can say with Paul, who wrote to the Roman Christians in their ongoing crisis situations:

Who shall separate us from the love of Christ? Shall trouble or hardship or persecution or famine or nakedness or danger or sword? [In other words, every crisis known to the world.] *As it is written: "For your sake we face death all day long; we are considered as sheep to be slaughtered."*

No, in all these things we are more than conquerors through Him who loved us. [We are overcomers.] *For I am convinced that neither death nor life, neither angels nor demons, neither the present nor the future, nor any powers, neither height nor depth, nor anything else in all creation, will be able to separate us from the* [unconquerable, ever-present] *love of God that is in Christ Jesus our Lord* (Romans 8:35-39).

Pay attention to the notes I added to these verses. For Kingdom people, these verses are important words. They express the message of this book—that there is no crisis too big for God. He will make sure that His people can conquer and overcome anything because His love is never overshadowed by any crisis.

Points to Ponder

The resources we need come to us in the natural course of living our lives according to God's design and intention.

Kingdom of God benefits come to us
as we seek the Kingdom.

The provisions and resources that we need
are by-products of our faith.

Kingdom-dwellers have faith.

True Kingdom people treat their faith
as a relationship with an invisible King.

Your King has made blessings accessible to
all who have eyes to see and ears to hear.

Words of Wisdom

You never know how much you really believe anything until its truth or falsehood becomes a matter of life and death to you.

—C.S. Lewis

Lord, keep me safe because I trust in You. My soul said You are my Lord, apart from You I have nothing to hope for. Those who worship earthly gods will never find peace; I will not worship idols nor confess them with my lips. Lord You are my future inheritance; You are my satisfaction who will protect me in death.

—Elmer L. Towns, *Praying the Heart of David*[1]

And he charged them, saying, Thus shall ye do in the fear of the Lord, faithfully, and with a perfect heart (2 Chronicles 19:9 KJV).

Now, as always, God discloses Himself to "babes" and hides Himself in thick darkness from the wise and the prudent. We must simplify our approach to Him. We must strip down to essentials (and they will be found to be blessedly few). We must put away all effort to impress, and come with the guileless candor of childhood. If we do this, without doubt God will quickly respond.

—A.W. Tozer

Faith begins by embracing what God has freely provided in the form of righteousness. Faith and righteousness are always connected. That's why Romans 1:17 says, "...*The righteousness of God is revealed from faith to faith*...." It is a progressive revelation of righteousness. This gift begins to go into operation as it is revealed to your heart.

—Faisal Malick, *Positioned to Bless*[2]

MY WISDOM KEYS

_____

_____

_____

_____

_____

_____

_____

_____

_____

_____

_____

_____

_____

7

Wisdom of Change

Some people do not like change. But even those people realize that seasonal change has many benefits. They understand that the earth needs a rest between growing seasons. It needs to gather nutrients and become ready for the coming growing season. They understand that times of plenty, while they may be followed by times of lack, will be followed again in due time by more seasons of plenty. They appreciate the different kinds of beauty that accompany each of the seasons.

God established the seasons of the year. He is the one who created climate differences. He made the tropics, and He made Antarctica. He made the oceans, and He made the mountains. He is the founding Father of seasonal change.

(Excerpts from *Overcoming Crisis*)

Wisdom Reflections

NOTHING is permanent *except God and His promises.* The leaves may fall from the trees, and the weather may change, but God never changes. He is the same yesterday, today, and forever (see Heb. 13:8).

God, the Unchanging One, is the One who set up the ever-changing seasons of the earth and of our lives. And He knew what He was doing. For one thing, He wanted His people to understand that they do not need to worry about their lives. Whatever is happening is not permanent. God is in charge of all of the changes. Therefore, it does not matter what is happening because it cannot last. There will be an end to every crisis.

It does not matter if what is happening seems good to you or if it seems bad because it will change eventually, and your God orchestrates the changing. Seasons are His way of guaranteeing improvement. This means that seasonal change is one of His most consistent ways of bringing *hope.* This means that you do not throw your hope away, even in the darkest season of your life. After all, no matter how cold you get in the winter, you always know summer is coming. Likewise, when winter comes, you do not throw away your swim trunks. You know the summer will come around again. You know you will need those swim trunks—but when you jump in the water to go swimming, you will not need the long-sleeved pullover you may have been wearing in the middle of the winter.

In the same way, when a "wintery" economic season comes upon you, do not throw away your bank account, even if it seems useless. Leave some money in it to keep it open. Why? Because the season is coming when you will be able to add more money to it again. Everything is seasonal, times of plenty and times of poverty. Winter never stays. Summer never stays, either.

Both employment and unemployment are seasonal. If you are unemployed, then a time of employment lies ahead. If this is the season for you to leave your job, then a better job is up ahead. You have got to close out one chapter in order to open up the next one. Most of the time, you have to get ready for a chapter that is bigger and better than the one before.

To everything there is a season. Times of crisis are temporary. This is good.

Points to Ponder

God is the same yesterday, today, and forever
(see Heb. 13:8).

God is in charge of all changes.

It does not matter what is happening because it will not last.

There will be an end to every crisis.

Everything is seasonal, times of plenty and times of poverty.

Are you open to change?

Words of Wisdom

There is a time for everything,
and a season for every activity under heaven:

a time to be born and a time to die,
a time to plant and a time to uproot,

a time to kill and a time to heal,
a time to tear down and a time to build,

a time to weep and a time to laugh,
a time to mourn and a time to dance,

a time to scatter stones and a time to gather them,
a time to embrace and a time to refrain,

a time to search and a time to give up,
a time to keep and a time to throw away,

a time to tear and a time to mend,
a time to be silent and a time to speak,

a time to love and a time to hate,
a time for war and a time for peace (Ecclesiastes 3:1-8).

MY WISDOM KEYS

_____

_____

_____

_____

_____

_____

_____

_____

_____

_____

_____

_____

8

Wisdom Seeds

By means of the Seed Principle, God sustains life. If the seeds are managed properly, life will not die out. Season after season, everything will grow and bear more fruit.

Jesus taught us to pray, "Give us this day our daily bread," but as you know, God doesn't have any bread growing on trees. He does not give us bread outright; He gives us seed. He gives us wheat, oats, barley, and other kinds of seeds that reproduce enough seed kernels to be put through a grinding process to make flour, which is then made into bread.

(Excerpts from *Overcoming Crisis*)

Wisdom Reflections

I T is good to know the Seed Principle when we pray for something and His answer does not seem to resemble what we prayed for. We know God does not make mistakes. Could it be that He has supplied us with the *seed* we need? Could it be that we need to patiently tend the seed until it reproduces? Could some kind of grinding (in the form of crises) be involved in the process of producing, at long last, the thing you prayed for?

You prayed for money, and He gave you a job. Well, there you go; your hard work is the cultivation process. You will reap the money you prayed for. You prayed for the harvest, the end product. That is not a bad thing to pray for. But do not be surprised when the answer you get is in the form of harvest-producing seed. God may deploy you to sow some seed and to take care of it until it grows up. Then you can have your harvest, and with it comes the idea of sowing some more seed.

You prayed that you would be a true citizen of the Kingdom. Instead of transforming you instantly into a fully mature believer, He just sent you a crisis. What is happening? Out of the midst of the fire, He intends to purify you. He wants you to come out shiny and strong, so that you can, like a true citizen of the Kingdom, reproduce Kingdom life generously.

God does not give you ready-to-eat bread. He gives you seed. This shows that He is a wise Father. You know as well as I do what happens when we just give a handout of bread to a beggar.

It may take care of him for one day, but what about tomorrow? Once he eats the bread, he is back to begging for more. Far better to help that beggar earn a living so he can acquire his own bread. It may take quite awhile, but it will be a better result.

Do not allow it to remain a mere seed. It is important for you to find it, plant it, and nurture it to maturity. Assuming that you do this, your seed will multiply greatly.

Points to Ponder

God does not make mistakes.

Do not be surprised when God's answer
is in the form of harvest-producing seed.

Out of the midst of the fire, God purifies you.

Find God's seed for you. Plant it. Nurture it to maturity.

Your seed will multiply greatly.

Words of Wisdom

This seeding of culture with the tools necessary for recognizing Him is not unique to the Hawaiian culture. It is typical of how God prepares people from their foundation for the living out of their destiny. It is just as typical that He sends people from outside of the culture to trigger His revelation in its fullness.

—James Wilson, *Living as Ambassadors of Relationships*[1]

I tell you the truth, unless a kernel of wheat falls to the ground and dies, it remains only a single seed. But if it dies, it produces many seeds (John 12:24).

What would happen if tens of thousands of hundreds of thousands of spiritual fathers and mothers in America and beyond committed themselves to prayer and fasting for the breaking of the spirit of Jezebel over their lives and the lives of their children [seeds]? ...What would happen? Nothing short of a revolution.

—James W. Goll and Lou Engle, *The Call of the Elijah Revolution*[2]

Although God desires to bless His people and use them to bless the earth, the devil always seeks to destroy. ...That is why he has so savagely attacked the family, sowing seeds of discord, distrust, and moral confusion that lead to divorce, broken lives, broken relationships, and shattered hopes and dreams.

—James W. Goll and Lou Engle, *The Call of the Elijah Revolution*[3]

My Wisdom Keys

_____

_____

_____

_____

_____

_____

_____

_____

_____

_____

_____

_____

_____

9

Wisdom Working

Your *job* is what you were trained to do. You may have gone to school to learn your job. On your job, you have certain duties, and you get paid for doing them. But as you well know, your employer can always find somebody else who has been trained to do that particular job, or your boss can decide that a person is no longer needed to do that job. All too easily, you can be replaced, laid off, or fired. Sometimes the company you work for will fail and close its doors, causing you and all of your fellow employees to lose your jobs.

But your *work* is different.

(Excerpts from *Overcoming Crisis*)

Wisdom Reflections

YOUR work is what you were born to do. No kind of educational system can teach you your true work because it is your life purpose, and it is revealed by your God-given gifts. No employer on earth can take that away from you. Nobody can fire you from that. They can lay you off from a job, but they cannot lay you off from being yourself. When you leave a job, you take your work, which is your innate purpose, with you. Wherever you land, you can plant your giftedness so that it can start to grow again. You are much more than your job.

We all need to think about our jobs, and we need to put effort into satisfying the requirements of our jobs. But we also need to think about our true work, our purpose in life, our God-given assignment. Whether you are currently job-hunting or happily employed, you should spend just as much time trying to find your*self* as you spend trying to find a job or satisfy the people you work for. Shift your thinking. If you can find your*self*, you will gain a new perspective on what you were created to do on this earth.

You were not created to punch a time clock. That's just what you may happen to be doing at the beginning and end of your workdays. You were created to contribute to the great bringing-in of the Kingdom of God. The King created you, and the King called you. He gave you special gifts that match with His purpose for your life. He wants you to discover that purpose so that you can fulfill it.

Fulfilling your God-given purpose can happen wherever you go. By God's grace, you can do your *work* even if you are "out of work" at the moment. God likes to move people around. He makes sure that He has representatives in many places, and that includes as many workplaces and job categories as possible, including the "unemployed" category. Your work is ongoing, throughout your life on this planet.

Your job is only your career. It is temporary. You can lose it. Your whole career can collapse. You can also have more than one career in your lifetime. But your work is your life assignment. You cannot lose that. Yes, you can let it languish, unexplored and untried, but you cannot lose the assignment you were born with. You cannot be deprived of your innate gifts and life purpose even if you are deprived of a paying job for a long time.

Points to Ponder

Your job is what you were trained to do.
Your work is different.

You are much more than your job.

If you can find yourself, you will gain a new perspective
on what you were created to do on this earth.

The King created you, and the King called you.

He gave you special gifts that match with
His purpose for your life.

He wants you to discover that purpose
so that you can fulfill it.

Words of Wisdom

There are too many people who feel locked in the wrong job. They hate getting up in the morning and heading off to work. They find no joy in their work. Here is the good news. You don't have to stay in that dungeon. There are keys to finding the right job for you.

—Noel Jones and Scott Chaplan, *Vow of Prosperity*[1]

Thus the heavens and the earth were completed in all their vast array. By the seventh day God had finished the work he had been doing; so on the seventh day he rested from all his work (Genesis 2:1-2).

Twentieth-century man needs to be reminded at times that work is not the result of the Fall. Man was made to work, because the God who made him was a "working God." Man was made to be creative, with his mind and his hands. Work is part of the dignity of his existence.

—Sinclair Ferguson[2]

I long to accomplish great and noble tasks, but it is my chief duty to accomplish humble tasks as though they were great and noble. The world is moved along, not only by the mighty shoves of its heroes, but also by the aggregate of the tiny pushes of each honest worker.

—Helen Keller

MY WISDOM KEYS

10

Wisdom in Serving

You were created to be deployed. You were created to serve the world around you with Kingdom compassion and Kingdom energy. The Kingdom of God is characterized by a culture of servanthood, and Jesus is the foremost example of this kind of servanthood. He both modeled it and taught it. He explained to His disciples that they should not look for status or high position and that they should not lord it over other people, but rather serve others.

(Excerpts from *Overcoming Crisis*)

Wisdom Reflections

IN Jesus' words, "Whoever wants to become great among you must be your servant, and whoever wants to be first must be your slave." Someone who is "first" is the first one whom people call on when they have a need. A person who is "great" may or may not hold a political office or some worldly leadership position, but that person is seen as hardworking and dependable.

Are people always asking you for help? If so, you should take it as a good sign that you are reflecting the character of your King. If not, it may be time to take a close look at your attitude, your work habits, and your motivations. Maybe people can tell that you are not inclined to serve and that, in fact, you are rather self-focused. Maybe they can tell that instead of reaching out to others, you tend to hold back or even to demand services from them.

What is another way that you can be sure that you are reflecting the King's character and that you have a true heart of service? Look at your attitude toward work. Do you shoulder your share of the work without murmuring or complaining? If so, then you have probably already been deployed in the service of the King. You probably already know that being a servant is not a bad thing. Far from indicating that you are merely subservient, finding joy in your work indicates that you have found your God-given gift (or gifts) and that you are willing to share what He has given you with the world around you.

And that alone is enough to make you "great" in the Kingdom of God.

The Kingdom of God operates in a most unique way. It is the only kingdom anywhere that designates every single citizen as a king in his or her own right. You are a king, and I am a king. The person who sat next to you at last week's worship service is a king, too.

This is a high privilege and an honor. Being a king also carries with it a built-in expectation that you and I will spend all of the days of our lives serving. We are servant kings. We work our way up the Kingdom management ladder by working our way down in lowly service. We are kings who serve the world with our God-given gifts.

Points to Ponder

You were created to serve the world around you with
Kingdom compassion and Kingdom energy.

If people are always asking you for help,
you must be reflecting the character of your King.

If you shoulder your share of the work
without murmuring or complaining,
then you have probably already been
deployed in the service of the King.

God's Kingdom designates every single citizen
as a king in his or her own right.

You work your way up the Kingdom management ladder
by working your way down in lowly service.

You are a king who serves the world
with your God-given gifts.

Words of Wisdom

You don't have to serve God long to be tempted to think your work is in vain. Thoughts come that your service is a waste of time. Results are hard to find. Regardless of what you think and see, God promises that your work is never in vain (1 Corinthians 15:58). That doesn't mean you'll ever see all the fruit of your labors you'd hope for, or that you won't frequently feel nothing has come of all your efforts. But it does mean that even if you can't see proof, your service to God is never in vain.

—Donald Whitney, *Spiritual Disciplines for the Christian Life*[1]

Jesus called them together and said, "You know that the rulers of the Gentiles lord it over them, and their high officials exercise authority over them. Not so with you. Instead, whoever wants to become great among you must be your servant, and whoever wants to be first must be your slave—just as the Son of Man did not come to be served, but to serve, and to give His life as a ransom for many" (Matthew 20:25-28).

When I went to New York, I had nothing; nothing, that is, except a willingness to obey God and go. I obeyed though I had nothing. I have watched over the years as God has faithfully blessed every new step that I have taken. ...Now, we're purchasing an entire city block that encompasses five office buildings. ...I took a measure of faith 20 years ago to step out and buy that building when we had only $98.16. It's the same today; it still takes faith to step out [to serve].

—Bill Wilson, *Christianity in the Crosshairs*[2]

My Wisdom Keys

_____

_____

_____

_____

_____

_____

_____

_____

_____

_____

_____

_____

_____

11

Wisdom's Secret

Every human is searching for the simple formula to a successful, fulfilled life. They want to find the one key that unlocks the door to the good life and answers the questions of their heart. Perhaps this is why *The Secret* became a sudden best-selling book even though its reign was short lived. This book promised the final key to life and success. (I was amazed to find, when I read this book, that it was simply a restatement of all the principles already written in the Bible and the same material I and many others have been sharing for years. In essence, the secret was never a secret.)

(Excerpts from *Applying the Kingdom*)

Wisdom Reflections

IF you conducted a sidewalk poll in any city, anywhere in the world, and asked people, "What is the key to life?" you would get many different answers. Some would say the key to life is to make as much money as you can, as quickly as you can, and to hold onto it as long as you can. Others would see gaining political power and influence as the key to life. Love would be the key for many.

Then there are always those who would say that there is no key to life. Life is an accident; it just happened and therefore has no key or significance. The fact is, most people don't know the key to life. This is why so many people live tragic lives; they don't know why they are here. They haven't a clue about how to make their time on this earth count for something worthwhile. Their existence is, in many ways, a kind of "living death" because a life without purpose is not really a life at all.

So what is the key to life? Finding your true purpose and living it. I know the word purpose has been almost over-used in recent years, and many think they understand it, but I wish to advise that this most essential component in life has never and can never be exhausted. Let me sum this up in four statements that all relate to purpose—four "keys" to understanding the difference between a purpose-filled life and a life with no meaning.

The greatest tragedy in life is not death, but life without a purpose. Many people today are obsessed with finding ways to prolong their lives. They are so caught up with trying to live longer that they never stop to consider why they are living at all. Drifting from one day to the next without purpose, with untapped potential and unfulfilled dreams; this is for many a fate worse than death. The rising suicide rate in modern society bears this truth out. Many people, bereft of hope, take their own lives because they find death more appealing than continuing what is to them a meaningless existence. Finding our purpose in life is critically important.

Points to Ponder

"What is the key to life?"

Is love the key?

Is life just an accident?

Is your existence a kind of "living death"?

Finding your true purpose and living it is the key to life.

The greatest tragedy in life is not death,
but life without purpose.

Words of Wisdom

But I have raised you up for this very purpose, that I might show you my power and that my name might be proclaimed in all the earth (Exodus 9:16).

❧

Control your own destiny, or someone else will.

—Jack Welch

❧

So do not be ashamed to testify about our Lord, or ashamed of me his prisoner. But join with me in suffering for the gospel, by the power of God, who has saved us and called us to a holy life—not because of anything we have done but because of his own purpose and grace. This grace was given us in Christ Jesus before the beginning of time (2 Timothy 1:8-9).

❧

You are not an accident. Your birth was no mistake or mishap, and your life is no fluke of nature. Your parents may not have planned you, but God did. He was not at all surprised by your birth. In fact, he expected.

—Rick Warren, *The Purpose Driven Life*[1]

❧

It is not in the stars to hold our destiny, but within ourselves.

—William Shakespeare

MY WISDOM KEYS

_____

_____

_____

_____

_____

_____

_____

_____

_____

12

Wisdom Focus

Every human heart longs for a simple life. We are naturally attracted to people who exhibit a focused, purposeful, organized life and simplified lifestyle. I believe this is the fundamental attraction of millions to the man Jesus Christ. There has never been a character who displayed such a strong spirit of personal conviction, purpose, self-awareness, confidence, self-worth, and a sense of destiny as this one man. The most impacting aspect of His life was His clear sense of priority.

(Excerpts from *Applying the Kingdom*)

Wisdom Reflections

JESUS Christ is the most focused and single-minded person who has ever lived. His entire life on earth was dedicated to one theme—the Kingdom of Heaven. Even by the age of 12 Jesus already knew His life purpose and priority. When His earthly parents, relieved at finding Him in the temple in Jerusalem after searching diligently for Him for three days, chided Him for worrying them, He said, *"Why were you searching for me? Didn't you know I had to be in my Father's house?"* (Luke 2:49). Another way to phrase the same question: *"Did you not know that I must be about My Father's business?"* (Luke 2:49 NKJV). Already Jesus had a singular focus on His Father's priority, and He never lost sight of it.

It was, in part, this singularity of purpose and clarity of priorities that caused Jesus to stand out so clearly among the people of His day. Unlike Jesus, people in general have a problem putting first things first. When man lost his dominion in the Garden of Eden he also lost his sense of proper priority and purpose. In fact, all humanity wrestles with two parallel problems related to priority: either absence of priority or misplaced priority. Both carry significant consequences.

Absence of priority causes one to drift through life with no focus or sense of purpose or direction. All of one's energy and potential are dissipated by trying to shoot off in too many directions and trying to do too many things. In many cases, people with no priority become lethargic and apathetic. A dull sameness characterizes their day-to-day living.

Misplaced priority results in wasting one's life pursuing the wrong thing, carrying out the wrong assignment. People with misplaced priority may be very focused individuals, but they are focused on the wrong thing. A life absent of priority accomplishes nothing in the end, while a life of misplaced priority may succeed in many things, but not in that which is most important. Either way, the end result is a failed life.

Do you want to come to the end of your days only to look back and have to say, regretfully, "I failed"? I know I don't!

Points to Ponder

Do you long for a focused, purposeful, organized life
and simplified lifestyle?

Do you have a problem putting first things first?

Are you drifting through life with no focus
or sense of purpose or direction?

Do you shoot off in too many directions trying
to do too many things?

Are you focused on the wrong thing?

What can you do today to better prioritize your life?

Words of Wisdom

So when they saw Him, they were amazed; and His mother said to Him, "Son, why have You done this to us? Look, Your father and I have sought You anxiously." And He said to them, "Why did you seek Me? Did you not know that I must be about My Father's business?" (Luke 2:48-49)

⌒

In space, astronauts experience the misery of having no reference point, no force that draws them to the center. Where there is no "moral gravity"—that is, no force that draws us to the center—there is spiritual weightlessness. We float on feelings that will carry us where we were never meant to go; we bubble with emotional experiences that we often take for spiritual ones; and we are puffed up with pride. Instead of seriousness, there is foolishness. Instead of gravity, flippancy. Sentimentality takes the place of theology. Our reference point will never serve to keep our feet on solid rock. Our reference point, until we answer God's call, is merely ourselves. We cannot possibly tell which end is up.

—Elizabeth Elliot

⌒

It is time for you to take charge of your spiritual life. One of the devil's tactics is to make people believe they have no choice in the direction of their lives. Having no voice in your own affairs is like playing a baseball game without knowing where the bases are!

—Billy Joe Daugherty, *When Life Throws You a Curve*[1]

⌒

You must never allow your human weakness to disqualify you for what God has planned for you. Your failures do not prove that you are wicked; they simply prove that you are human. Though you are filled with God, it's important to remember that you're a human being who is filled with God.

—Don Nori, *The Prayer God Loves to Answer*[2]

79

MY WISDOM KEYS

_____

_____

_____

_____

_____

_____

_____

_____

_____

_____

_____

_____

_____

13

Wisdom to Prioritize

Nothing is more tragic than a life without purpose. Why is purpose so important? Purpose is the source of priorities. Defining our life's priorities is extremely difficult unless we first discover and define our purpose. Purpose is defined as the original reason and intent for the creation of a thing. Therefore, purpose is the source of meaning and significance for all created things.

If purpose is not known, priorities cannot be established and nothing significant or worthwhile in life can be accomplished. In essence, if you don't know why you are on planet Earth and posses a clear sense of purpose and destiny, the demand for priorities is low or nonexistent.

(Excerpts from *Applying the Kingdom*)

Wisdom Reflections

THE truth is, if you don't know where you are going, any road will take you there. Life is daily and constantly demanding of our time, energy, talent, attention, and focus. Therefore, to effectively manage the everyday demands, we must know what our priorities are. No matter what we think about life, we have to live it every day and give an account of our management.

I believe the greatest challenge in life is the daily demand to choose between competing alternatives that consume our lives. If we do not have clear and correct priorities in our lives and know what we should be doing, our lives will be an exercise in futility. The absence of priority is dangerous and detrimental.

Absence of priority results, first of all, in the wasting of time and energy. If you're not doing the right thing at the right time, that means you are doing the wrong thing at the wrong time. But you expend the same time and energy either way. Time and energy, once spent, are gone forever. They cannot be replaced.

When priority is absent, you become busy on the wrong things. If you don't know what the right things are, you will end up focusing on the wrong things. These "wrong things" may not be bad or evil in themselves; they are just wrong for you because they will distract you from pursuing your life purpose.

People without priority spend their time doing the unnecessary. If you think about it, most of what we do on a daily basis is not really necessary. We spend most of our time sweating, fretting, and laboring over issues that, in the eternal scheme of things, are pointless. And in the meantime, the things that really matter go undone.

In a similar way, absence of priority causes people to major on the unimportant. If you have no priority, you end up majoring on the minors. For some reason most of us are easily distracted or enticed away from focusing on the most important matters in life to concentrate instead on peripheral issues. Proverbs 29:18a says, *"Where there is no revelation* [vision], *the people cast off restraint."* Priority helps us sharpen our vision so we can focus on the most important things. Without it, we have no sense of direction and are apt to pursue whatever suits our fancy at the time.

Points to Ponder

If you don't know where you are going,
any road will take you there.

Life is daily and constantly demanding of our time,
energy, talent, attention, and focus.

You must know what your priorities are.

The absence of priority is dangerous and detrimental.

If you're not doing the right thing at the right time,
you are doing the wrong thing at the wrong time.

Prioritizing sharpens your vision so you
can focus on the most important things.

Words of Wisdom

God longs to be loved. He wants to know that He is more important than revival. He must be more of a priority than the multitudes, than the fruit, than the miracles. When we are that in love with Him, fruit happens. It is effortless in love.

—Dr. Heidi Baker, *God's Supernatural Power*[1]

But seek first His kingdom and His righteousness, and all these things will be given to you as well (Matthew 6:33).

A true faith in Jesus Christ will not suffer us to be idle. No, it is an active, lively, restless principle; it fills the heart, so that it cannot be easy till it is doing something for Jesus Christ.

—George Whitefield

Secondly, rejoicing, praying, and thanksgiving are all acts of our will that, particularly in times of difficulty, weakness, and uncertainty, require faith. They are activities that draw our focus to Heaven so we can agree with what is true, no matter what we feel or perceive with our physical senses and emotions.

—Bill Johnson, *Strengthen Yourself in the Lord*[2]

Satan's greatest success is in making people think they have plenty of time before they die to consider their eternal welfare.

—John Owen

MY WISDOM KEYS

_____

_____

_____

_____

_____

_____

_____

_____

_____

_____

_____

_____

_____

_____

_____

14

Wisdom and Obedience

A continuing hunger and thirst for righteousness positions us to enter into the fullness of Kingdom life. Remember that righteousness is a legal term that means to be in alignment with authority; to be in right standing with the governing power. The key to maintaining that right standing is obedience to the laws of that government. In a kingdom, since the king's word is law, righteousness means fulfilling the king's requirements. Our pursuit of righteousness places us in the right positioning to receive all the rights, resources, blessings, and privileges of the Kingdom that are ours as Kingdom citizens.

(Excerpts from *Applying the Kingdom*)

Wisdom Reflections

IN this positioning there is a part we play and a part that God plays. Our part is to obey the laws of the government, thus keeping ourselves in alignment. God's part is to open up to us the resources of Heaven. It is a very simple dynamic. We obey, God opens; we disobey, He closes. As long as we obey the law, we have access. As soon as we disobey—get out of alignment—that access shuts down. This explains why so many believers struggle from day to day, pinching pennies, trying to make ends meet, but never seem to have enough, with no peace, joy, or contentment. They are out of alignment with their government, and their access to Kingdom resources has been shut off.

Whenever this happens, it is always due to sin, which is breaking the law. The literal meaning of the Greek word for sin in the New Testament is to "miss the mark." It is an archery term that refers to falling short of the target. Sin interrupts our communication with God and shuts down the flow of His resources to us. As the psalmist said, *"If I regard iniquity in my heart, the Lord will not hear"* (Ps. 66:18 NKJV). *Iniquity* is another word for *sin,* but refers specifically to invisible sin, such as greed, envy, lust, and hatred, and is worse than physical sin. Invisible sin is secret sin, which gives rise to visible sins of action.

Righteous positioning means keeping our hearts pure— clean and uncorrupted by iniquity. If we harbor no secret sins in our heart, there will be nothing to give rise to visible sins. Purity of heart is a critical, indispensable key to abundant Kingdom life. Jesus said, *"Blessed are the pure in heart, for they will see God"* (Matt. 5:8). Literally, this means that the pure in heart will see God in everything. The word *heart* in this verse means "mind." If our minds are pure, we will see God in everything and in everyone. This is the answer to the problem of greed, or lust, or jealousy, or any kind of impure or improper thought or attitude.

What a challenge to live at such a level in our world today! But that is just the challenge that the King calls His citizens to take up, a challenge that we can meet successfully in His mighty power. But we must choose the path of righteousness and be in the right positioning with regard to our King's requirements. We must be in the position to receive His favor.

Points to Ponder

The key to maintaining right standing is obedience.

Your pursuit of righteousness places you in the right
positioning to receive all the rights, resources,
blessings, and privileges of the Kingdom.

It's very simple: you obey, God opens;
you disobey, He closes.

Sin interrupts your communication with God
and shuts down the flow of His resources to you.

If your mind is pure, you will see
God in everything and in everyone.

Words of Wisdom

Instant obedience is the only kind of obedience there is; delayed obedience is disobedience.

—Thomas a Kempis

I prayed to the Lord my God and confessed: "O Lord, the great and awesome God, who keeps His covenant of love with all who love Him and obey His commands (Daniel 9:4).

My mother used to say, when her six children were misbehaving, "I'm not talking to hear myself think!" Neither is God. When He speaks to you every day, He has a purpose. God wants to tell you to change something or encourage you, to change or encourage your friends, to change the Church, or to change the world.

—Steve Shultz, *Can't You Talk Louder God?*[1]

Dear friends, if our hearts do not condemn us, we have confidence before God and receive from Him anything we ask, because we obey His commands and do what pleases Him. And this is His command: to believe in the name of His Son, Jesus Christ, and to love one another as He commanded us (1 John 3:21-23).

MY WISDOM KEYS

_____

_____

_____

_____

_____

_____

_____

_____

_____

_____

_____

_____

_____

_____

15

Wisdom, Righteousness, Generosity

Righteousness bears abundant fruit in our lives. One of these is a spirit of generosity, along with the means and capacity to give generously. Jesus said, *"It is more blessed to give than to receive"* (Acts 20:35b), and Paul reminds us that, *"God loves a cheerful giver"* (2 Cor. 9:7b).

Generosity is a character trait of the righteous, of those who are positioned properly with the government of God. After all, if we own nothing and are merely stewards of God's property, there is no reason why we cannot give freely. And if we are heirs to the Kingdom of God and all its riches, which are infinite, we can give with no fear of running out.

(Excerpts from *Applying the Kingdom*)

Wisdom Reflections

THE prosperity of the righteous is an ongoing blessing from God that spans generations. David writes,

I was young and now I am old, yet I have never seen the righteous forsaken or their children begging bread. They are always generous and lend freely; their children will be blessed (Psalm 37:25-26).

God never forsakes the righteous or their children. He always provides for them. The fruit of the righteous extends even beyond their lifetime to bless their children. Righteous living will bear the fruit in our lives of an inheritance we can leave to our descendents. We should be so blessed that our children, grandchildren, nieces, nephews, and cousins should inherit a multiplied blessing, all because we lived our life rightly positioned with God's government. That is the kind of fruit He wants to give us.

Right positioning places us under the protection of the King, who will preserve us even when the wicked are destroyed:

For the Lord loves the just and will not forsake His faithful ones. They will be protected forever, but the offspring of the wicked will be cut off; the righteous will inherit the land and dwell in it forever (Psalm 37:28-29).

Ultimately, the real estate of the Kingdom is reserved for the righteous, for those who are lined up with the Kingdom government. The destiny and prosperity of the ancient Israelites were intimately connected to the land. Even today, the only true material wealth of any lasting value, particularly as an inheritance to pass on, is real estate. A fancy house doesn't matter. A fancy car doesn't matter. The best designer label clothes don't matter. These things rust, rot, and fall apart. If you want to leave your children and grandchildren a valuable legacy, leave them land, not things. Leave them also the legacy of your example of not laying up treasures on earth, which pass away, but treasures in Heaven, which last forever (see Matt. 6:19-20).

Not only will the righteous inherit land to dwell in forever, but that land will be covered by a peace and security that the world knows nothing about:

> *The fruit of righteousness will be peace; the effect of righteousness will be quietness and confidence forever. My people will live in peaceful dwelling places, in secure homes, in undisturbed places of rest* (Isaiah 32:17-18).

What an incredible threefold promise!

Points to Ponder

Righteousness bears abundant fruit in your life.

Generosity is a character trait of the righteous.

God never forsakes the righteous or their children—
He always provides for them.

Righteous living will bear the fruit in your life of
an inheritance you can leave to your descendents.

The only true material wealth of any lasting value,
particularly as an inheritance to pass on, is real estate.

Not only will the righteous inherit land to dwell in forever,
but that land will be covered with peace and security.

Words of Wisdom

Seek ye the Lord while He may be found, call ye upon Him while He is near: let the wicked forsake his way, and the unrighteous man his thoughts: and let him return unto the Lord, and He will have mercy upon him; and to our God, for He will abundantly pardon (Isaiah 55:6-7 KJV).

God sends no one away empty except those who are full of themselves.

—D.L. Moody

I am afraid there are Calvinists, who, while they account it a proof of their humility that they are willing in words to debase the creature, and to give all the glory of salvation to the Lord, yet know not what manner of spirit they are of. Whatever it be that makes us trust in ourselves that we are comparatively wise or good, so as to treat those with contempt who do not subscribe to our doctrines, or follow our party, is a proof and fruit of a self-righteous spirit. Self-righteousness can feed upon doctrines, as well as upon good works; and a man may have the heart of a Pharisee, while his head is stored with orthodox notions of the unworthiness of the creature and the riches of free grace.

—John Newton

Even in darkness light dawns for the upright, for the gracious and compassionate and righteous man (Psalm 112:4).

The more excellent something is the more likely it will be imitated. There are many false diamonds and rubies, but who goes about making counterfeit pebbles? However, the more excellent things are the more difficult it is to imitate them in their essential character and intrinsic virtues. Yet the more variable the imitations be, the more skill and subtlety will be used in making them an exact imitation. So it is with Christian virtues and graces. The devil and men's own deceitful hearts tend to imitate those things that have the highest value. So no graces are more counterfeited than love and humility. For these are the virtues where the beauty of a true Christian is seen most clearly.

—Jonathan Edwards, *Religious Affections*

MY WISDOM KEYS

16

Wisdom and God's Big Idea

The world is ruled by dead men. This statement may surprise you, but after a little thought, you would likely agree when you consider that all of the ideologies that serve as the foundations of all governments, religions, and social and civic institutions are built on dead men's ideas. Imperialism, monarchism, socialism, communism, democracy, and dictatorship are all born of ideas cultivated, incubated, and developed by men who, though long laid to rest, still live on in the practice of these ideas in our modern societies.

(Excerpts from *God's Big Idea*)

Wisdom Reflections

OUR planet spins under the power of ideas, and these ideas are the source of the conditions on this Earth. Consider this: every government in every nation is guided and regulated by ideas. All laws and legislation are products of ideas, and the social and cultural standards in all communities throughout the world are results of ideas that societies have embraced as acceptable and thus manifested in social behavior.

An idea was introduced to the Earth by the Creator of the Earth and was lost soon after the beginning of the human journey—and has ever since been the object of the search of the human spirit. This idea originated in the mind and heart of the Creator and was the motivation and purpose for the creation of the physical universe and the human species. This "Big Idea" is superior to all the collective wisdom and ideas of human intellect. It is an idea that is beyond the philosophical reserves of human history and supersedes the institutions that govern mankind since his first human society.

The "big idea" is not a new idea. It has been imitated, disguised, misused, misinterpreted, and misunderstood by mankind throughout history and still seems to elude the wisest among us.

What is this "big idea"? The big idea is the ideology that served as the foundation of the first and original government instituted on Earth. It is the divine aspiration, celestial vision, and eternal purpose of the Creator for His creation and humanity on planet Earth. The big idea is the concept of the ultimate governing program for mankind on Earth that provides for all the fundamental needs of humanity and produces a culture that integrates all the noble aspirations of all mankind, such as equality, justice, peace, love, unity, and respect for human dignity, human value, and personal and corporate empowerment. It is an idea that is superior to and contains all the noble aspirations of democracy, socialism, communism, imperialism, dictatorships, and all religions. It is my hope that unveiling the beauty of this great idea will bring the solutions to all of our earthly problems—problems such as war, terrorism, crime, AIDS epidemics, child abuse, environmental destruction, culture clashes, poverty, oppression, ethnic cleansing, economic crisis, family disintegration, political and religious corruption, community violence, and the culture of fear.

Points to Ponder

The world is ruled by dead men.

Our planet spins under the power of ideas.

The big idea is the ideology that served as the foundation of the first and original government instituted on Earth.

The big idea is the divine aspiration, celestial vision, and eternal purpose of the Creator for His creation and humanity on planet Earth.

The big idea is the concept of the ultimate governing program for mankind on Earth that provides for all the fundamental needs of humanity and produces a culture that integrates all the noble aspirations of all mankind, such as equality, justice, peace, love, unity, and respect for human dignity, human value, and personal and corporate empowerment.

Words of Wisdom

When God breathed into Adam, he received the power to reach his potential. The mere form of man became a living soul. The word *living* means to be vibrant, alive, and strong. You have great potential in your life.

—T.D. Jakes, *Release Your Anointing*[1]

And yet His work has been finished since the creation of the world. For somewhere He has spoken about the seventh day in these words: "And on the seventh day God rested from all His work" (Hebrews 4:4).

The church is going to be putting aside petty theological differences anyway, and getting back to God. Overall, what's on the horizon will be a much more spiritual age, with the heavy chains of rationalism lifted.

—John Crowder, *The New Mystics*[2]

Some in the Church today are aware that God is doing something new. He seeks to raise up a new order of things. This new order includes a new understanding of the Tabernacle in us to hold the glory of God. ...What God is creating in us today may not have been seen in the past on the scale that it will come forth. To accomplish this sovereign work, one thing God is doing in the Church today is killing religion.

—Francis J. Sizer, *Into His Presence*[3]

MY WISDOM KEYS

_____

_____

_____

_____

_____

_____

_____

_____

_____

_____

_____

_____

17

Wisdom of Ideas

I believe in this "big idea" so deeply, and testify of its evidence in my own life experience, that I have dedicated my entire life to propagating it, spreading it around, and sharing it with every human I encounter.

This idea is not religious dogma or some narrow theological stance that isolates one from the rest of the human family. Rather, it supersedes any religious institutional position and defies the limited boundaries of all other philosophies and ideologies of mankind. This big idea is so pure that it conflicts with all of our learned theses and leads us to a frontier that appeals to the better nature of mankind.

(Excerpts from *God's Big Idea*)

Wisdom Reflections

WHAT is this idea? It's the divine conception of the colonization of Earth by the Kingdom of Heaven, which impacts Earth's territory with the loving culture of Heaven on Earth, producing a colony of citizens who exhibit the nature, values, morals, and lifestyle of Heaven on Earth. This is not a religious idea, but a global invasion of love, joy, peace, goodness, kindness, justice, patience, and righteousness under the influence of the heavenly governor: the Spirit of God.

It is the idea that humankind can be restored to the original passion, purpose, and plan of the Creator to extend His heavenly Kingdom, the celestial country, to Earth as a colony of Heaven through mankind and thus fill the Earth with His divine nature manifested in all human behavior. This is not religion, but the manifestation of a government from another realm. What an idea! It's the Big Idea.

Death can never kill an idea. Ideas are more powerful than death. Ideas outlive men and can never be destroyed. As a matter of fact, ideas produce everything. Everything began as an idea and is the result of the conception of an idea. This book itself is the result of an idea, and the paper on which it is printed used to be an idea. The shoes on your feet, the clothes on your back, the house in which you live, the car you may drive, the cup from which you drink, and the spoon you use were all just ideas that were delivered by some human effort.

The most difficult thing to fight against is an idea! Philosophically speaking, ideas can never be destroyed by physical weapons such as swords, guns, tanks, nuclear weapons, or biological/chemical weapons. Ideas may have a shelf life, but can never be extinct. Why? Because they incubate in a place where no weapon can reach: the mind. If you kill a man, you do not destroy his ideas. Ideas can be transferred and live on for generations.

Points to Ponder

Death can never kill an idea.

Ideas are more powerful than death.

Ideas outlive men and can never be destroyed.

Everything began as an idea and is the result
of the conception of an idea.

The most difficult thing to fight against is an idea!

Ideas can be transferred and live on for generations.

Words of Wisdom

Great ideas often receive violent opposition from mediocre minds.

—Albert Einstein

For My thoughts are not your thoughts, neither are your ways My ways, declares the Lord. As the heavens are higher than the earth, so are My ways higher than your ways and My thoughts than your thoughts (Isaiah 55:8-9).

A man may die, nations may rise and fall, but an idea lives on. Ideas have endurance without death.

—John Fitzgerald Kennedy

In the face of unbelief, you must stand strong when you know that God has moved in your life. Don't let the enemy or even well-meaning people defeat you! They will confuse you and cause you to doubt yourself and God.

—Leigh Valentine, *Successfully You!*[1]

The idea of saying, "Why aren't you like me?" is no longer a question in our hearts. We realize that we need each other to be exactly who God created us to be. We no longer pick on each other's weaknesses. Instead, we partake of our strengths and enjoy one another.

—Joyce Meyer, "Everyday Answers: Two Are Better Than One"[2]

MY WISDOM KEYS

_____

_____

_____

_____

_____

_____

_____

_____

_____

_____

_____

_____

_____

18

Wisdom and the Master Gardener

We need to stop allowing the wrong person to tend our garden. It is time to change both our thinking and our behavior to bring them in line with who we really are. Christ set us free. Through His death and resurrection, He cleansed us of our sin—our rebellion against God—and gave us access to His Kingdom. Then He gave us the Governor to teach us how to live as Kingdom citizens. The Governor, the Holy Spirit, is the Master Gardener who ensures that the gardens of our lives produce good fruit that is appropriate and pleasing to the King, to whom the gardens belong. Could there be any greater freedom—or any greater destiny—than this?

(Excerpts from *God's Big Idea*)

Wisdom Reflections

THIS question of who tends our garden is vitally important because whoever tends the garden controls the fruit. Whoever tends our garden determines our culture, our values, our beliefs, and our behavior. God created us. He fashioned our bodies from the dust of the ground and breathed His life into us. We belong to Him; we are His house. The devil wants to take up residence in us through demonic powers, because he knows that once he is inside he can work through us to wield his evil influence at home, at school, at work, at church, in the neighborhood, in the community, and even in the nation.

We were created to be filled with the Spirit of God and to live in perfect harmony and fellowship with Him, not to be under the thumb of a demonic pretender exercising illegitimate authority. This is why, whenever Jesus encountered a demonic spirit possessing a human being, He cast out the spirit: illegal residence. As believers, we have a choice as to who we allow to tend our garden. One choice leads to a wasted and unfulfilled life while the other leads to great abundance and fullness of life.

We have been trained by religion to be scared of the devil. Most of our churches have taught us to regard the world situation as hopeless, to prepare ourselves to leave, and then to pray for the Lord to rescue us out of this world. Having conceded victory to the pretender, we feel that all we can hope to do is

112

circle the wagons and defend ourselves as best we can until Christ comes back and takes us away. We have become a bunch of holy sissies. Not only is this an unnecessarily pessimistic and defeatist mind-set, it also runs contrary to the expressed will and purpose of our King.

Points to Ponder

God is the Master Gardener who ensures that
the gardens of our lives produce good fruit.

Whoever tends your garden determines your
culture, values, beliefs, and behavior.

Has the devil taken up residence in you?

You were created to be filled with the Spirit of God
and live in perfect harmony and fellowship with Him.

You have a choice as to who you allow
to tend your garden.

Are you a holy sissy?

Words of Wisdom

Your heart should be thumping in your chest and your blood should be racing like a car engine, knowing that God will soon bring about a great harvest in your life.

—Millicent Hunter, *Don't Die in the Winter*[1]

Peacemakers who sow in peace raise a harvest of righteousness (James 3:18).

We need to keep our hearts like we keep a garden. We must not put off the need for weed-pulling. Our repentance must be immediate each time we see a weed of sin emerging. It is our responsibility to get out there and pull those weeds.

—Don Nori Sr., *Manifest Presence*[2]

Of Mans First Disobedience, and the Fruit
Of that Forbidden Tree, whose mortal tast
Brought Death into the World, and all our woe,
With loss of EDEN, till one greater Man
Restore us, and regain the blissful Seat,
Sing Heav'nly Muse, that on the secret top....

—John Milton, *Paradise Lost*[3]

MY WISDOM KEYS

19

Wisdom Through Temptation

We are so in the habit of being afraid of the devil that whenever any kind of trial or trouble comes along we immediately assume it is a demonic attack. We earnestly pray to the Lord to deliver us without ever considering the possibility that the trial may have come for the purpose of strengthening our faith and helping us to grow toward spiritual maturity. James, the brother of the Lord Jesus, wrote:

Consider it pure joy, my brothers, whenever you face trials of many kinds, because you know that the testing of your faith develops perseverance. Perseverance must finish its work so that you may be mature and complete, not lacking anything (James 1:2-4).

(Excerpts from *God's Big Idea*)

Wisdom Reflections

D O the words in James 1 sound like someone who fears the enemy or someone who is getting ready to "skip town," expecting to be taken out of the world at any moment? No, these are the words of someone determined to occupy until the Lord comes (see also Luke 19:13 KJV). For those who do occupy and stand firm, a rich reward lies in store:

> *Blessed is the man who perseveres under trial, because when he has stood the test, he will receive the crown of life that God has promised to those who love Him* (James 1:12).

Temptation is a fact of life in a fallen world. For Kingdom citizens, however, temptation does not have to mean fear or failure, but can be the catalyst for strengthening and growth. Satan tempts with the intent to destroy, but Kingdom citizens have an advantage not available to those outside the Kingdom; the King Himself places a limit on how much temptation He allows us to face. As the apostle Paul wrote to the believers in the city of Corinth:

> *No temptation has seized you except what is common to man. And God is faithful; He will not let you be tempted beyond what you can bear. But when you are tempted, He will also provide a way out so that you can stand up under it* (1 Corinthians 10:13).

If our King will not allow us to be tempted beyond what we can bear, that means that whatever temptations we *do* face, we *can* bear, as long as we do so in His strength rather than our own. The Governor is always with us, and His strength is readily available to us, so we need not fear anything the devil tries to do to us. God is committed to the glory of His name, the growth of His Kingdom, and the good of His children, and He will do whatever is necessary to turn everything to serve His divine purpose, even the evil efforts of the enemy.

Points to Ponder

Are you afraid of the devil?

Temptation is a fact of life.

Satan tempts with the intent to destroy.

If you occupy and stand firm during temptations,
a rich reward lies in store for you.

Your King will not allow you to be
tempted beyond what you can bear.

Whatever temptations you *do* face, you *can* bear, as long as
you do so in His strength rather than your own.

Words of Wisdom

Temptation often comes wrapped in the form of something beautiful, something that appeals to our senses and desires. It is often necessary to think twice before we recognize that a beautiful object or goal (at times) is really sin in disguise.

—Henry Virkler, *Hermeneutics*[1]

꙰

No man knows how bad he is till he has tried very hard to be good. A silly idea is current that good people do not know what temptation means. This is an obvious lie. Only those who try to resist temptation know how strong it is. After all, you find out the strength of the German army by fighting it, not by giving in. A man who gives in to temptation after five minutes simply does not know what it would have been like an hour later. That is why bad people, in one sense, know very little about badness. They have lived a sheltered life by always giving in. We never find out the strength of the evil impulse inside us until we try to fight it.

—C.S. Lewis, *Mere Christianity*[2]

꙰

Watch and pray so that you will not fall into temptation. The spirit is willing, but the body is weak (Matthew 26:41).

꙰

Let no man think himself to be holy because he is not tempted, for the holiest and highest in life have the most temptations. How much higher the hill is, so much is the wind there greater; so, how much higher the life is, so much the stronger is the temptation of the enemy.

—John Wycliffe

MY WISDOM KEYS

20

Wisdom in the Kingdom of Heaven

By now it should be abundantly clear that the Kingdom of Heaven is not a religion and has nothing at all to do with religion. In Eden, the original Kingdom Garden on Earth, there was no religion. There was no worship in the sense that we usually understand the word. Adam and Eve enjoyed full, open, and transparent fellowship and interaction with their Creator in a mutual relationship of pure love with absolutely no guilt, shame, or fear. Their disobedience broke that relationship, and humanity's efforts to restore it on their own without divine assistance gave rise to religion.

(Excerpts from *God's Big Idea*)

Wisdom Reflections

THE Kingdom of Heaven is the sovereign rulership of the King (God) over a territory (Earth), impacting it with His will, purposes, and intent, producing a citizenry of people (ekklesia—the Church) who express a culture reflecting the nature and lifestyle of the King. Therefore, the Kingdom of Heaven is a real, literal country, although invisible to physical eyes because it is spiritual in nature. As King of Heaven, God's big idea was to extend the influence of His heavenly country over and throughout the Earth. So we are really talking about two things here: God's country and its influence.

In reading the four Gospels of the New Testament—Matthew, Mark, Luke, and John—it becomes immediately clear that Jesus used two similar but different phrases to refer to the country of the King and the influence of the King. Sometimes He referred to the "Kingdom of Heaven," and at other times to the "Kingdom of God." Although it is common to use these phrases interchangeably, there is an important difference in focus. The phrase "Kingdom of Heaven" refers to the literal place, the "headquarters" country of God. "Kingdom of God," on the other hand, refers to the King's influence wherever it extends, but especially its extension into the earthly realm.

The most powerful expression of any nation is its culture: its values, morals, customs, codes of conduct, standards of living, modes of dress, food, and dietary practices, etc. A strong and rich culture can wield an influence far beyond its geographical boundaries. France is a good example. Historically, French culture has a high and proud heritage with truly worldwide influence, particularly in the areas of language and the culinary arts. Many English words—"croissant" for example—either were borrowed directly from the French or are of French origin or derivation. French cooking is deservedly famous around the world and so influential that even to this day most of the terminology used in Western cooking is French (such as sauté). One reason French culture has had such tremendous influence is because Louis XIV, the "Sun King," was the most powerful monarch in European history. The culture of his kingdom spread not only throughout Europe, but also to all nations worldwide that were originally colonized by European nations. So, even though the kingdom of Louis XIV is long gone, the influence of its culture remains.

Points to Ponder

The Kingdom of Heaven is not a religion and
has nothing at all to do with religion.

The Kingdom of Heaven is the sovereign rulership
of the King (God) over a territory (Earth).

The Kingdom of Heaven is a real, literal country, although
invisible to physical eyes because it is spiritual in nature.

The most powerful expression of any nation is its culture.

A strong and rich culture can wield an influence
far beyond its geographical boundaries.

Are you spreading the culture of the Kingdom of Heaven?

Words of Wisdom

We must make the invisible kingdom visible in our midst.

—John Calvin

Jesus answered, "I tell you the truth, no one can enter the kingdom of God unless he is born of water and the Spirit" (John 3:5).

I place no value on anything I have or may possess, except in relation to the kingdom of God. If anything will advance the interests of the kingdom, it shall be given away or kept, only as by giving or keeping it I shall most promote the glory of Him to whom I owe all my hopes in time or eternity.

—David Livingstone

Lord, when I pray, I'll follow this pattern: My Father in Heaven, may Your name be holy, In my life on earth as Your name is holy in Heaven. May Your Kingdom come in my life on earth as Your will is done in Heaven.

—Elmer L. Towns, *Praying the Gospels*[1]

My Wisdom Keys

_____

_____

_____

_____

_____

_____

_____

_____

_____

_____

_____

_____

_____

21

Wisdom's Influence

There are two kinds of influence: the influence of the moment, which spreads rapidly and then disappears just as quickly; and lasting influence, which grows more slowly, but succeeds through persistence and permeation. Momentary or fleeting influence includes such fads as fashion, hairstyles, and the latest "popular" books, which are here today and gone tomorrow. These superficial influences, and others like them, may make a big stir in society for a time, but they generally lack the depth and substance to effect any significant changes in the culture. Influence that lasts operates more subtly and works from the inside out, altering external appearances and behavior by changing internal values, beliefs, and mind-sets.

(Excerpts from *God's Big Idea*)

Wisdom Reflections

KINGDOM influence is of the second type. It operates gradually, based on eternal, unchanging principles of God and according to a timetable that encompasses millennia. God literally has all the time in the universe to fulfill His plan. Consider this: at least 4,000 years passed from the time Adam and Eve lost the kingdom in Eden until Christ announced its return. More than 2,000 years have elapsed since Jesus walked the Earth, and God's ultimate plan has still not yet reached completion. But throughout all that time, His influence has been growing and expanding gradually and sometimes almost invisibly, permeating human culture. And none of the efforts of either humans or the pretender can stop it.

Ultimately, the influence of God's Kingdom is irresistible. This does not mean that everyone eventually will enter the Kingdom, but it does mean that someday everyone will acknowledge the reality, authority, and absolute supremacy of the Kingdom of Heaven. The apostle Paul stated plainly that the day will come when "*at the name of Jesus every knee should bow, in heaven and on earth and under the earth, and every tongue confess that Jesus Christ is Lord, to the glory of God the Father*" (Phil. 2:10-11). The word *Lord* means "owner" and is a term properly applied to a king. Christ is the King of an eternal, all-powerful, all-knowing, present-everywhere Kingdom, and one day everyone will confess that this is so, even those who have rejected His Kingdom.

The Kingdom of Heaven is so subtle and unassuming in its growth that many people ignore it or dismiss it altogether as completely inconsequential. Eventually, however, it will grow to be revealed to everyone as it really is: the greatest Kingdom of all, next to which the kingdoms of man are nothing.

> *...The kingdom of heaven is like yeast that a woman took and mixed into a large amount of flour until it worked all through the dough* (Matthew 13:33).

Anyone who spends any amount of time in the kitchen knows what yeast is and what it does (knowing how it does what it does is another matter). Yeast is one of the most powerful influencing agents in the world, and it exists for one reason: to infect whatever it is mixed into with its presence and influence. Jesus' comparison of the Kingdom of Heaven to yeast makes us think right away about impact.

Points to Ponder

There are two kinds of influence: the influence
of the moment and lasting influence.

Kingdom influence operates gradually, based on eternal,
unchanging principles of God and according to
a timetable that encompasses millennia.

The influence of God's Kingdom is irresistible.

Christ is the King of an eternal, all-powerful,
all-knowing, present-everywhere Kingdom.

Yeast is one of the most powerful
influencing agents in the world.

Are you influencing others for the Kingdom of God?

Words of Wisdom

You are the only Bible some unbelievers will ever read, and your life is under scrutiny every day. What do others learn from you? Do they see an accurate picture of your God?

—John MacArthur

By the blessing of the influence of the upright and God's favor [because of them] the city is exalted, but it is overthrown by the mouth of the wicked (Proverbs 11:11 AMP).

Someone has said that more is learned from what is "caught" that "taught"....Though it is certainly important to communicate God's Word didactically, it's what people see in our lives that gives weight to our words. That is why the qualifications for elders are so important. If we are to "teach the Word of God" effectively, we must simultaneously "live the Word of God."

—Gene Getz, *Elders and Leaders*[1]

Whenever I hear anything spoken in conversation of any person, if I think it would be praiseworthy in me, Resolved to endeavor to imitate it.

—Jonathan Edwards, *Resolution Number 54, July 8, 1723*

MY WISDOM KEYS

22

Wisdom Against Rebellion

In the Bible, rebellion against God is called sin. This is exactly what Adam and Eve were guilty of in the Garden of Eden. Their deliberate defiance of God's prohibition against eating the fruit of the tree in the center of the Garden was an act of open rebellion. In so doing they were exercising their free will, the freedom to choose that God had given them. Before free will can truly exist, there must also be a component of choice, because free will is only possible where there is an alternative. So the tree in the center of the Garden, and God's prohibition against eating its fruit, provided Adam and Eve with the capacity to use a gift that God had given them. Unfortunately, they used it in the wrong way; they could have freely chosen to obey God rather than disobey.

(Excerpts from *God's Big Idea*)

Wisdom Reflections

ADAM and Eve declared rebellion against the government of Heaven, and the Bible calls it sin. In fact, the Bible speaks in some instances of sin, singular, and in others, of sins, plural, and there is a difference. Sin is the singular act of rebellion, while sins are the manifestations of that one act. Rebelling against the Kingdom is sin; sins are the day-to-day actions that constitute rebel-like behavior. The declaration of independence of the Adamic race from the Kingdom of God was an act of rebellion that has caused all of us, like Adam, to go our own way.

This personal independence is the number one tenet of capitalism and democratic republics. The thing God hates is the very thing we magnify. The thing that God says is our condemnation is the very thing we regard as our highest achievement. As independent individuals we can do whatever we like and pursue our own happiness and our own joy at our own expense. We take great pride in "doing our own thing," while God says, "That's the very problem with the world." It's a paradox. This is why it is very difficult to live in the Kingdom of God and live at the same time in a democracy under a capitalistic system. It is hard to strike a balance between the two because the principles that operate them are diametrically opposed to each other. It is for this reason that many believers do not manifest Kingdom culture and values in their lives the way they should. In their struggle between the Kingdom and the world, the world usually wins.

Jesus Christ came to Earth to put an end to our sin of rebellion, and, through His blood, to cleanse us of our sins, the rebellious behavior that was the inevitable consequence of our sin. Christ came as a "second Adam" to reverse the consequences of the first Adam's failure.

Christ came to announce the return of the Kingdom of Heaven and to give us access through the sin-cleansing power of His blood. But He also, through His Spirit, placed in us the capacity to manifest Kingdom culture and values in our everyday life so that, as we go about our daily affairs, we can transform our little corner of the world into a thriving garden of His Kingdom.

Points to Ponder

Rebellion against God is called sin.

Sin is the singular act of rebellion, while sins are the manifestations of that one act.

Adam and Eve could have freely chosen to obey God rather than disobey Him.

Jesus Christ came to Earth to put an end to our sin of rebellion through His blood.

Christ came as a "second Adam" to reverse the consequences of the first Adam's failure.

Christ came to announce the return of the Kingdom of Heaven and to give us access through the sin-cleansing power of His blood.

Words of Wisdom

One day Jesus was on a mountain and He began to preach and teach what we know as the Beatitudes. I believe these "Beatitudes" are the attitudes we need to be in. They are attitudes that will teach us how to receive and dispense the Kingdom of God.

—Lynn Hiles, *The Revelation of Jesus Christ*[1]

...Sin entered the world through one man, and death through sin, and in this way death came to all men, because all sinned.... Consequently, just as the result of one trespass was condemnation for all men, so also the result of one act of righteousness was justification that brings life for all men. For just as through the disobedience of the one man the many were made sinners, so also through the obedience of the one man the many will be made righteous (Romans 5:12,18-19).

As a result of grace, we have been saved from sin's penalty. One day we will be saved from sin's presence. In the meantime we are being saved from sin's power.

—Alistair Begg, *Made For His Pleasure*[2]

For the first time in all eternity, the unity between God the Father and God the Son would be broken. This is because Jesus would become sin for us. God's eyes are too holy and pure to even look upon sin. So Jesus knew that the Father would have to turn His face from Him. This is what Jesus was agonizing over. To bypass the cross was His greatest temptation. Yet He said, "Nevertheless, not My will Father, but Yours be done."

—Richard Booker, *Living in His Presence*[3]

Y WISDOM
KEYS

23

Wisdom and Jesus

I believe no one who has ever lived has been misunderstood more than the young teacher who happened to be born, not by preference but by promise, through the line of the Old Testament Hebrew patriarch Abraham—Jesus the Christ. Misunderstanding Jesus has caused Muslims to reject Him, Hindus to suspect Him, Buddhists to ignore Him, atheists to hate Him, and agnostics to deny Him. But it just may be those who claim to represent Him the most—Christians—who have in fact misunderstood and, therefore, misrepresented Him the most.

(Excerpts from *Kingdom Principles*)

Wisdom Reflections

IF my statement in the opening page of this chapter sounds outlandish and way off the mark to you, let me encourage you to read on before closing your mind to this possibility. In my own life I have had to come to grips with my own personal defects related to my understanding of Jesus and His message. Everything Jesus said and did—His prayers, teachings, healings, and miracles—was focused on a kingdom, not a religion. Jesus was preoccupied with the Kingdom; it was His top priority, His heavenly mandate.

Those to whom He came first, the Jews, misunderstood Jesus and saw Him as a rebel, a misfit, and a fanatic. In their minds He was, at best, a misguided rabbinical teacher spreading heresies that contaminated the teachings and laws of Moses and Judaism. In truth, they had reduced the message of Moses to a sophisticated religion where strict observance of the laws became more important than the original purpose for those laws. And they expected Jesus to do the same. The original intent of God's mandate to Moses was not to establish a religion, but a nation of people who would love, serve, and honor God— *"a royal priesthood* [and] *a holy nation"* (1 Pet. 2:9).

The Muslim misunderstands Him as simply another in a line of prophets who was a great teacher, a good man, and a great prophet, but who fell short and failed to deliver the finished work of redemption to mankind.

The Hindu misunderstands Him as a good teacher, a good man, and just another deity to add to their list of gods to provide a service in their need for spiritual security.

The atheist, agnostic, and humanist see him as a mere man, an historical figure, whom a group of misguided men transformed into a god and an object of worship. They acknowledge that Jesus existed, but deny any of His miracles as well as His claim to divinity.

The media, scientists, and secularists see Him as fair game for investigation and criticism. They acknowledge Him as an interesting subject for arguments, theories, discussion, and debates while ignoring His divine claims and questioning His validity, integrity, and sometimes, His very existence.

Christians have misunderstood Him as the founder of a religion and have transformed His teachings and His methods into customs and His activities into rituals. Many even have reduced His message to nothing more than an escapist plan for getting to Heaven and His promises as a mere fire insurance policy for escaping the pains of a tormenting hell.

Points to Ponder

Everything Jesus said and did—His prayers, teachings, healings, and miracles—was focused on a kingdom, not a religion.

Have you had to come to grips with your own personal defects to understand Jesus and His message?

The original intent of God's mandate to Moses was not to establish a religion, but a nation of people who would love, serve, and honor God.

Do you understand Jesus?

Have you reduced His message to nothing more than an escapist plan for getting to Heaven and His promises as a mere fire insurance policy for escaping the pains of a tormenting hell?

Words of Wisdom

Jesus and His disciples went on to the villages around Caesarea Philippi. On the way He asked them, "Who do people say I am?" They replied, "Some say John the Baptist; others say Elijah; and still others, one of the prophets." "But what about you?" He asked. "Who do you say I am?" Peter answered, "You are the Christ" (Mark 8:26-29).

ᴄᴘ

Jesus knew intuitively that Peter was not able to answer that question because of a learned background in Messianic teachings. ...You can't see who Jesus is. You just have to know who He is by the Spirit. If the Spirit doesn't reveal it to you, then you cannot know, because God is never recognized, but revealed.

—Noel Jones, *God's Gonna Make You Laugh*[1]

ᴄᴘ

The significant thing is this: not one recognized religious leader in the history of the world has ever laid claim to being God—except Jesus. Moses did not. Paul was horrified when people tried to worship him. Muhammad insisted that he was merely a prophet of Allah. Buddha did not even believe in the existence of a personal God, and Confucius was skeptical. Zoroaster was a worshiper, but he was not worshiped. We repeat—of the recognized religious leaders of all time, Jesus of Nazareth—and Jesus of Nazareth alone—claimed to be eternal God.

—John H. Gerstner, *Theology for Everyman*[2]

ᴄᴘ

We believe in one Lord, Jesus Christ, the only Son of God, eternally begotten of the Father, God from God, light from light, true God from true God, begotten, not made, of one Being with the Father.

—Nicene Creed

MY WISDOM KEYS

24

Wisdom, Religion, Government

The power of religion lies in its ability to serve as a substitute for the Kingdom and thus hinder mankind from pursuing the genuine answer to his dilemma. My study of the nature of religion and how it impacts the process of man's search for the Kingdom uncovered several significant truths:

- Religion preoccupies man until he finds the Kingdom.
- Religion is what man does until he finds the Kingdom.
- Religion prepares man to leave earth; the Kingdom empowers man to dominate earth.
- Religion focuses on Heaven; the Kingdom focuses on earth.
- Religion is reaching up to God; the Kingdom is God coming down to man.
- Religion wants to escape earth; the Kingdom impacts, influences, and changes earth.
- Religion seeks to take earth to Heaven; the Kingdom seeks to bring Heaven to earth.

(Excerpts from *Kingdom Principles*)

Wisdom Reflections

IT seems clear from these words that religion is one of the greatest obstacles to the Kingdom. Perhaps this may be cause for us all to take another look at the power of religion over our lives, culture, and society.

Christianity as a religion is well-known, well-established, well-studied, well-researched, well-recorded, and well-distributed; but little or nothing is known about the Kingdom. As a matter of fact, most of those trained in official institutions to understand the Christian faith and propagate its purported message graduate without ever taking a single course in Kingdom studies. Often, no such course is available. The result is that few so-called ordained ministers and priests have any formal instruction at all in any Kingdom concept. Their priority is in propagating the Christian religion rather than the message and concepts of the Kingdom of God.

This perpetuation of the Christian religion and its rituals, customs, and rites has left a great vacuum in the world that must and can be filled only by understanding the Kingdom.

Throughout history, man's greatest challenge has been to learn how to live in peace with himself and his neighbors. Whether it is the continent of Africa, Old Europe, Norsemen of England, the Mongols of Asia, Indians of North and South America, or the Eskimos of Iceland, tribal warfare, racial and ethnic conflicts, and full-scale war have been the human story. In all of these social and cultural expressions of humanity, the one thing that has always evolved was some kind of authority structure, a form of leadership or government mechanism to establish and maintain social order.

From the painted walls of native caves and the hieroglyphics of the tombs of ancient Egypt, to the historic pyramid structures of the Aztec worshipers, evidence abounds of man's desire and need for some form of governmental structure. The need for government and order is inherent in the human spirit and is a manifestation of a divine mandate given to mankind by the Creator. Man was created to be a governor and ruler, and therefore, it is his nature to seek some authority mechanism that would bring order to his private and social world. Government is necessary, desirable, and essential to man's social context no matter how primitive or modern. This is why man continues to search for an effective way to govern himself.

Points to Ponder

Religion is one of the greatest obstacles to the Kingdom.

Few pastors have any formal instruction at all
in any Kingdom concept.

Humankind's greatest challenge has been
to learn how to live in peace.

The need for government and order is inherent in the
human spirit and is a manifestation of a divine mandate.

Man was created to be a governor and ruler.

It is in man's nature to seek some authority mechanism
that brings order to his private and social world.

Words of Wisdom

Of the increase of His government and peace there shall be no end, upon the throne of David, and upon His kingdom, to order it, and to establish it with judgment and with justice from henceforth even for ever. The zeal of the Lord of hosts will perform this (Isaiah 9:7).

Why do authorities exist? It is because we live in a sinful and fallen world, and without authority everyone would do "what is right in his own eyes," resulting in chaos. Those who will not be constrained from within by the living presence of Jesus Christ, must be restrained from without by the state, acting under God's ultimate authority, in order to "promote the general welfare," in the words of the Constitution's preamble.

—Cal Thomas, *The Authority of the State*[1]

The wealth of the West has created a society with a lingering cloud of tempting distractions. Because our society offers many options, people have filled up their time with more and more things in hope that they would find satisfaction and joy. The result is that people are busier than ever—busy from pursuing so many distractions.

—Robert Stearns, *Prepare the Way (or Get Out of the Way!)*[2]

At the same time, however, the kind of trust that we are called to give to our fellow imperfect humans in this life, be they family or friends, employers or government officials, or even leaders in a church, can never finally be earned. It must be given as a gift—a gift in faith, in trust more of the God who gives than of the leaders He has given (see Eph. 4:11-13).

—Mark Dever, *Nine Marks of a Healthy Church*[3]

151

MY WISDOM KEYS

_____

_____

_____

_____

_____

_____

_____

_____

_____

_____

_____

_____

25

Wisdom of Democracy

Democracy is the best form of civil government as we know it because of its basic tenets and because of the checks and balances of the system. It is also built on the premise and principle of the "majority rule" and the protection of individual rights. Democracy has served our nations well in that it has given voice to the people and provides opportunity for broad-based participation in the political process by the people of a nation. Its checks and balances system further protects the masses from monopolization of power by one or by the few.

(Excerpts from *Kingdom Principles*)

Wisdom Reflections

DESPITE its advantages and benefits, however, democracy does come with a few crucial defects. One such defect is its fundamental and major principle of "majority rule." This defect is critical because even though it gives power to the majority of the people, at the same time it places morality, values, and the standards for law at the mercy of the majority vote, thus legitimizing the majority's values, desires, beliefs, aspirations, and preferences.

If the power of democracy is in the people, then "we the people" become the sovereign of our lives and corporate destiny, and thus become our own providential ruler and god. This is the reemergence and manifestation of the age-old philosophy of humanism. Humanism is simply man becoming his own measure for morality, judgment, and justice that places man at the mercy of himself. So no matter how educated man may become, he can lead himself only as far as he goes himself. The record of history and the present state of the world gives evidence that man left to himself makes a poor god. Therefore, democracy without accountability to one greater than the people is an exercise in moral roulette. Simply put, democracy without God is man's worship and elevation of himself and his own intelligence. What a tragedy!

Democracy cannot succeed without God any more than communism can succeed without God. God is not subject to our politics, nor can He be, but He has created His own political system and governmental structure which, as this book will demonstrate, is far superior to all forms of earthly government. From the Creator's perspective, life is politics, and He is the essence of life. In Him there is no distinction between government and spirituality. They are one and the same. The assignment given to the first man in the Garden of Eden was a political assignment given to a spirit being living in a flesh body. Therefore, in the context of the original biblical mandate, the concept of the separation of church and state or religion and government is a lofty idea that has no root in biblical logic or fact. The original biblical mandate provides no foundation for it.

Everyone is religious in the sense that they bring to life their moral convictions no matter what their religious claim. We all are political and religious. There can be no separation. You cannot legislate a dichotomy between a man and his belief system. Legislation itself is the result and manifestation of a belief system and moral judgment. Therefore, democracy can succeed only where there is a clear accountability to a moral code accepted by the majority as being good, civil, and right, and which serves as the anchor and foundation for national governance.

Points to Ponder

Democracy is the best form of
civil government as we know it.

Democracy is built on the premise and principle of
"majority rule" and the protection of individual rights.

From the Creator's perspective, life is politics,
and He is the essence of life.

In Him there is no distinction between
government and spirituality.

We all are political and religious.

Democracy can succeed only where there is
a clear accountability to a moral code.

Words of Wisdom

In America, we have a long history of valuing the concept of the separation of church and state. This idea historically referred to a division of labors between the church and the civil magistrate. However, initially both the church and the state were seen as entities ordained by God and subject to His governance. In that sense, the state was considered to be an entity that was "under God." What has happened in the past few decades is the obfuscation of this original distinction between church and state, so that today the language we hear of separation of church and state, when carefully exegeted, communicates the idea of the separation of the state from God. In this sense, it's not merely that the state declares independence from the church, it also declares independence from God and presumes itself to rule with autonomy.

—R.C. Sproul, *Statism*[1]

᙭

At this, the administrators and the satraps tried to find grounds for charges against Daniel in his conduct of government affairs, but they were unable to do so. They could find no corruption in him, because he was trustworthy and neither corrupt nor negligent (Daniel 6:4).

᙭

It cannot be emphasized too strongly or too often that this great nation was founded, not by religionists, but by Christians; not on religions, but on the gospel of Jesus Christ. For this very reason peoples of other faiths have been afforded asylum, prosperity, and freedom of worship.

—Patrick Henry

᙭

Furthermore the Lord stated, "These two churches [South Korea and Japan] cannot be separated. These two nations will arise as true apostolic churches and will plant houses of worship all over the world."

—Israel Kim, *Find Your Promised Land*[2]

MY WISDOM KEYS

_____

_____

_____

_____

_____

_____

_____

_____

_____

_____

_____

_____

_____

_____

_____

26

Wisdom and Purpose

When I studied art in college, one of the fundamental concepts I learned is always to see the end first and then work my way back. In other words, a good artist sees the finished product in his or her mind before beginning to paint or sculpt or draw. That is what it means to get the big picture—to see the end from the beginning and keep that end clearly in view throughout the creative process. Only then can the artist ensure that the finished product conforms to his or her original vision or design.

(Excerpts from *Kingdom Principles*)

Wisdom Reflections

A casual observer of any given phase of the process often cannot make any sense out of it because he or she lacks the big picture of the finished product that is in the mind of the artist. A few brush strokes on a canvas may mean nothing to someone watching the painter, but a good artist will know exactly what he is doing. He will know exactly where he is going and how to get there because he already sees the end result in his mind. He sees the big picture. That is why you should never judge an artist while he is working. It is only in the finished product that his full vision and intent can be seen.

Whether you are painting a picture, carving a sculpture, or building a house, it is critical to keep the big picture—the finished product—clearly in view. Otherwise, your original dream or vision will never be realized, and you will end up with something quite different from what you intended.

The biggest problem in our world today, including the religious world, is that we are so preoccupied with the phases that we cannot see the big picture. We are so caught up with our own little part—and with fighting and arguing with everybody else over their little part—that we have lost sight of our purpose. The most important thing in life is the big picture. But all we have are snapshots. Somewhere along the way humanity lost the big picture of our purpose, and all we were left with were tiny snapshots that provide only a narrow and very misleading impression of the whole. Long ago we lost the end of our existence. Now all we have to work with are disconnected means—futile pursuits with no significance.

Purpose defines the big picture. In other words, the big picture is the original purpose or intent of the artist or builder—the desired end result. What was God's purpose as the Artist who created humanity? What was the end result He desired? As Designer of the human race, what was God's original intent? This is a critical issue for us because without purpose, human life has no meaning or significance. And that is exactly what the philosophers of our day are saying: Human life has no purpose or significance, so each of us must create or derive meaning for our lives wherever we can find it. We have lost the big picture—God's original intent for mankind—and without it our lives are nothing more than disjointed phases that make no sense.

Points to Ponder

The big picture means to see the end
from the beginning throughout the creative process.

A good artist already sees the end result in his mind.

Purpose defines the big picture.

What was God's purpose as the Artist
who created humanity?

Without purpose, human life has
no meaning or significance.

Can you see the big picture?

Words of Wisdom

Now it is God who makes both us and you stand firm in Christ. He anointed us, set His seal of ownership on us, and put His Spirit in our hearts as a deposit, guaranteeing what is to come (2 Corinthians 1:21-22).

The use of means ought not to lessen our faith in God, and our faith in God ought not to hinder our using whatever means He has given us for the accomplishment of His own purposes.

—Hudson Taylor

You must lay down your life in exchange for the life and destiny that God has called you to. You can't treat your calling as temporary. You can't walk in a vision of convenience, and plan to walk away if it dries up. Where God plants you, you have to say, "You know what, God? I'm going to stay here until the day I die unless You release me. I'm in it for the long haul."

—Bruce Allen, *Promise of the Third Day*[1]

God will not judge anyone for failing to perform a duty if the person had no access to the knowledge of that duty. But even without the Bible, all people have access to the knowledge that we are created by God and therefore depend on Him for everything, thus owing Him the gratitude and trust of our hearts. Deep within us we all know that it is our duty to glorify our Maker by thanking Him for all we have, trusting Him for all we need, and obeying all His revealed will.

—John Piper, *Desiring God*[2]

MY WISDOM KEYS

_____

_____

_____

_____

_____

_____

_____

_____

_____

_____

_____

_____

_____

27

Wisdom and Potential

Your life has the potential to fulfill your purpose. If, however, you imprison that potential, you rob your life of its purpose and fulfillment. You and every other individual on this planet possess an awesome treasure. Too much of this treasure is buried every day, untapped and untouched, in the cemeteries of our world. Much talent, skill, and creativity have been lost to the world for want of a little courage. Many obscure men and women enter eternity pregnant with potential, with a still-born purpose.

Living with ability brings responsibility. Dying with ability reveals irresponsibility.

(Excerpts from *Releasing Your Potential*)

Wisdom Reflections

EVERYTHING in creation was designed to function on the simple principle of receiving and releasing. Life depends on this principle. What if the plants refused to release the oxygen they possess or if we human beings refused to release the carbon dioxide we produce? The result would be chaos and death for the entire planet. Unreleased potential is not only useless, it is dangerous both for the person or thing who failed to release it and for everything that lives with them. Dormant potential is not healthy, advantageous, safe, or effective. You must understand that your valuable deposit of potential was given to enrich the lives of others. When potential is kept, it self-destructs.

The tremendous potential you and I have been given is locked inside us, waiting for demands to be made on it. We have a responsibility to use what God stored in us for the good of the world. We dare not leave this planet with it. Many of us are aware of the ability we have inside, but we have been frustrated by our failure to release that ability. Some of us blame our historical circumstances. Others blame social status. Still others transfer the responsibility for their failure and frustration to their lack of formal education or their less than ideal opportunities.

Over the years, I have come to realize that no excuse can be given to justify the destruction of the seed of potential that God placed within you. You can become the man or woman you were born to be. You can accomplish the vision you saw. You can build that business you planned. You can develop that school you imagine. You are the only one who can stop you. No matter what your environment, you have the ability to change your attitude and your internal environment until they are conducive to the germination of your potential seed. The purpose of this material is to help you understand and appropriate the principles necessary for releasing your potential. You must not add to the wealth of the graveyard. You owe it to the next generation to live courageously so the treasure of your potential is unleashed. The world needs what God deposited in you for the benefit of your contemporaries and all the generations to follow.

Tap the untapped. Release the reservoir.

Points to Ponder

Your life has the potential to fulfill your purpose.

If you imprison that potential, you rob your life
of its purpose and fulfillment.

You possess an awesome treasure.

Your valuable deposit of potential was given
to enrich the lives of others.

You have the ability to change your attitude
and your internal environment until they are
conducive to the germination of your potential seed.

You owe it to the next generation to live courageously
so the treasure of your potential is unleashed.

Words of Wisdom

The Lord wants to help you realize who you are and what you are graced to do. When you understand that He is the only One who really knows you, then you pursue Him with fierceness and determination. Pursue Him!

—T.D. Jakes, *Can You Stand to be Blessed?*[1]

I am only one, but still I am one. I cannot do everything, but I can still do something; and because I cannot do everything, I will not refuse to do something that I can do.

—Helen Keller

To our renewed minds God can begin to reveal His will—the special plan that He has for the lives of each one of us. God's will is unfolded in three successive phases as our minds become more and more renewed.

—Derek Prince, *Faith to Live By*[2]

Continuous effort—not strength or intelligence—is the key to unlocking our potential.

—Winston Churchill

MY WISDOM KEYS

_____

_____

_____

_____

_____

_____

_____

_____

_____

_____

_____

_____

_____

28

Wisdom's Death

As silence answered, I suddenly applied the questions to the many tombstones that surrounded this child's resting place. Some of the others had recorded life spans of thirty, forty, sixty, and even seventy-five years. Yet the only testimony to their time on this planet was "Rest in Peace." Then I wondered: How can you rest in peace if you died with all your potential inside? As the wet, misty rain formed dew drops on my cheeks, I walked away thinking: What a tragedy it is for a child to die at such a tender age, before he has the opportunity to realize his full potential.

(Excerpts from *Releasing Your Potential*)

Wisdom Reflections

IMMEDIATELY a quiet voice screamed in my head: Is it not a greater tragedy if those who lived to old age also carried their books, art, music, inventions, dreams, and potential to the grave? Suddenly the rain seemed to turn to sweat as I pondered the awesome implications of this question. One of my greatest fears is that many who still walk the streets of our world, perhaps some who are reading this book, will also deposit in the cemeteries of their communities the wealth of potential locked inside them. I trust that you will not allow the grave to rob this world of your latent, awesome potential.

There are five billion people on this planet. Each one is very special, unique, original, and significant. All possess a genetic combination that codes them as distinct individuals whose fingerprints cannot be duplicated. There is no one like you now, nor will there ever be another. Each of us—whether black, brown, yellow, red, or white—was conceived by destiny, produced by purpose, and packaged with potential to live a meaningful, fulfilling life. Deep within you lies a seed of greatness waiting to be germinated. You have been endued with natural talents, gifts, desires, and dreams. All humanity, in all cultures, races, and socio-economic situations, lives with the natural instinct to manifest this potential.

The entire creation possesses this principle of potential. Everything has the natural instinct to release its ability. The plant and animal kingdoms abound with evidences of this fact. The Creator designed everything with this principle of potential, which can be simplified to the concept of a seed. The biblical document states that God created everything with *"seed in it according to their kinds"* (Gen. 1:12). In essence, hidden within everything is the potential to fulfill itself and produce much more than we see.

You have the ability to accomplish everything your God-given purpose demands. Your Creator has given you the responsibility of releasing this precious seed in obedience to His commands. The releasing of your potential is not up to God but you.

Points to Ponder

Don't allow the grave to rob this world
of your latent, awesome potential.

Deep within you lies a seed of greatness
waiting to be germinated.

You have been endued with natural talents,
gifts, desires, and dreams.

Hidden within everything is the potential to fulfill itself
and produce much more than you see.

You have the ability to accomplish everything
your God-given purpose demands.

The releasing of your potential is not up to God but you.

Words of Wisdom

One isn't necessarily born with courage, but one is born with potential. Without courage, we cannot practice any other virtue with consistency. We can't be kind, true, merciful, generous, or honest.

—Maya Angelou

You should be and are intended to be certain of His love and the redeeming power of His love to hold, forgive, and restore you. You need to spend your time, energy, anointing, and creativity fulfilling His dreams for you, not trying to simply stay saved. If you have the power to keep yourself saved, then you could have saved yourself without the blood of Jesus.

—Don Nori Sr., *The Love Shack*[1]

God has a plan for your life. However, that plan cannot come to pass until it is spoken. God chose to allow His only begotten Son to be born, to live, to die, and to be resurrected so He could restore man to his rightful place. God saw that plan with His own eyes of faith.

—Keith Hudson, *The Cry*[2]

...Be strong and of good courage, and do it; do not fear nor be dismayed, for the Lord God—my God—will be with you. He will not leave you nor forsake you, until you have finished all the work for the service of the house of the Lord (1 Chronicles 28:20 NKJV).

MY WISDOM KEYS

_____

_____

_____

_____

_____

_____

_____

_____

_____

_____

_____

_____

_____

29

Wisdom Abhors Abortion

Abortion is the ignorance of responsibility and the denial of obligation. Abortion is self-comfort at the expense of fruitfulness, because all abortions sacrifice responsibility. The abortion of potential condemns the future. This reality has caused the development of an entire discipline of science. Ecology and environmental studies, as these areas of concern are known, build their premises on the word extinction, meaning "the termination of the potential force within creation to fulfill itself."

(Excerpts from *Releasing Your Potential*)

Wisdom Reflections

IT is amazing that man, with all his attempts to minimize the abortion of various species in the animal and plant kingdom by investing billions of dollars to protect animals, plants, forests, and the ozone layer, has neglected to prioritize the position of human beings in the scheme of things. While man fights to protect whales, owls, trees, and fish, he also battles for the right to terminate human babies. Perhaps the situation would improve if every doctor who performs this tragic operation would be reminded before each abortion that the opportunity to perform this surgery is his only because his mother did not abort him.

The abortion issue is, therefore, not just a problem of the taking of a life, though that is the fatal end result. Even more, abortion is the ignorance and the lack of understanding of the principle of potential that pervades our world. The majority of those who die each year are guilty of abortion because they didn't understand the basic relevance of the concept of potential to their individual lives.

The abortion of potential is the death of the future. It affects generation after generation. When Adam broke God's law, he aborted his seed's potential for becoming all they were intended to be. Men and women throughout all ages have fallen far short of the glory of the Creator. The word *glory* means the "true nature, or full essence" of a thing. In other words, to fall short of glory means to live below your true potential. This is what God calls sin. Sin is not a behavior; it is a disposition. One of the great biblical writers states it this way:

I consider that our present sufferings are not worth comparing with the glory that will be revealed in us. The creation waits in eager expectation for [the glory of] *the sons of God to be revealed* (Romans 8:18-19).

This passage states that the fall of man prevented the full glory or true potential of mankind from being revealed or manifested. All creation was affected by man's sin. God's creation is waiting for man's glory or true potential to be exposed because creation's destiny is tied to man's. Thus, any abortion, whether it's the abortion of a dream, a vision, art, music, writing, business, leadership, or inventions, affects both nature and the succeeding generations of man.

Points to Ponder

Abortion is the ignorance of responsibility
and the denial of obligation.

Abortion is self-comfort at the expense of fruitfulness.

The abortion of potential is the death of the future.

Abortion is the ignorance and the lack of understanding of
the principle of potential that pervades our world.

All creation was affected by man's sin.

What are your thoughts about abortion?

Words of Wisdom

But when Jesus saw it, He was greatly displeased and said to them, "Let the little children come to Me, and do not forbid them; for of such is the kingdom of God (Mark 10:14 NKJV).

⌒

These concerns (for orphan children in India and elsewhere in the world) are very good, but often these same people are not concerned with the millions that are killed by the deliberate decision of their own mothers. And this is what is the greatest destroyer of peace today, Abortion....For the pregnant women who don't want their children, give them to me.

—Mother Teresa of Calcutta

⌒

Abortion is a violation of the supernatural laws of the spirit. When you take the life of your unborn child, you invite all kinds of devastation into your heart that can't necessarily be explained in words, but that will very much be experienced. This often results in symptoms like sickness, depression, fatigue, and a host of other negative conditions that are actually signs of a spiritual storm inside of you.

—Kris Vallotton, *Sexual Revolution*[1]

⌒

Worldwide:

- Number of abortions per year: Approximately 42 million
- Number of abortions per day: Approximately 115,000
- Where abortions occur: 83% of all abortions are obtained in developing countries and 17% occur in developed countries.

—www.abortionno.org[2]

MY WISDOM KEYS

_____

_____

_____

_____

_____

_____

_____

_____

_____

_____

_____

_____

_____

30

Wisdom From the Beginning

God also planted within you the ability to be much more than you are at any one moment. Like the apple seed, you possess hidden resources and capabilities. Most of the potential God gave you at birth still remains within you, unseen and unused. What I see when I meet you on any given day is not all you are.

(Excerpts from *Releasing Your Potential*)

Wisdom Reflections

EVERYTHING that was and is was in God. Before God created anything, there was only God. Thus, God had within Him the potential for everything He made. Nothing exists that was not first in God. God is the source of all life, because before anything was, God is.

"In the beginning God created the heavens and the earth" (Gen. 1:1). He pulled everything that He made out of Himself. Indeed, the beginning was in God before it began. God started start. If the Book of Genesis had started with Genesis 1:0, it might have read, "Before there was a beginning, there was God. Before there was a creation, there was a Creator. Before anything was, there was God."

God did not begin when the beginning began. He was in the beginning before the beginning had a beginning. *"In the beginning was the Word, and the Word was with God, and the Word was God"* (John 1:1). Everything in the world we know was in God before it came to be seen. *"Through [God] all things were made; without Him nothing was made that has been made"* (John 1:3). Thus, God is the source of all potential. He is everything we haven't seen yet.

God is always full of power. He can always do more than He has already done. God's process in creating the world follows an interesting pattern.

First, God planned what He wanted to create. Second, He decided what kind of material substance He wanted His creation to be made from. Third, God spoke to the substance from which the thing was to be created and, fourth, exactly what He spoke came forth from that to which He spoke.

Thus, when God wanted to make plants, He spoke to the ground, because that is the material substance from which He wanted them to come (see Gen. 1:11). When He wanted to create animals, God again spoke to the ground because He had planned for animals to be made of dirt (see Gen. 1:24). Fish came forth from the sea when God spoke to it (see Gen. 1:20). The sun, the moon, and the stars appeared in the expanse of the sky when God called them into being (see Gen. 1:14-17). Everything came forth when God spoke to a material substance, in accordance with the plan He had developed before He spoke the world into being.

Points to Ponder

Most of the potential God gave you at birth still remains within you, unseen and unused.

On any given day, you are not all you can be.

God can always do more than He has already done.

Everything came forth when God spoke it into a material substance, in accordance with His master plan.

What steps can you take to begin realizing your potential?

Can you see yourself in God's master plan?

Words of Wisdom

Before man can work he must have both tools and materials, but God began with nothing, and by His Word alone out of nothing made all things. The intellect cannot grasp it. God *"spake and it was done, He commanded and it stood fast"* (Ps. 33:9). Primeval matter heard His voice. *"God said, Let there be...and it was so"* (Gen. 1).

—A.W. Pink, *The Attributes of God*[1]

Then they said to Him, "Who are You?" And Jesus said to them, "Just what I have been saying to you from the beginning. I have many things to say and to judge concerning you, but He who sent Me is true; and I speak to the world those things which I heard from Him" (John 8:25-26 NKJV).

I've served God my whole life. I've gone to church my whole life. I've been a pastor for 10 years, but my spirit was awakened in the move of God that I was part of in Sarnia. My spirit was asleep, but now I'm different.

—Greg Holmes, *If He Builds It, They Will Come*[2]

The difficulty of the commands is merely a reflection of the greatness of the Gospel. Jesus' expectation is built on His anticipation of what God will do in the lives of His people! Jesus demands the humanly impossible precisely because His provisions are supernatural. The magnitude of Jesus' commands must mean, therefore, that they are tied to the grandest promise of all, namely, the promise that God himself will work in every circumstance to conform us to the image of Christ (see Rom. 8:28-29).

—Scott Hafemann, *The God of Promise and the Life of Faith*[3]

M Y WISDOM KEYS

_____

_____

_____

_____

_____

_____

_____

_____

_____

_____

_____

_____

_____

_____

31

Wisdom and Your Body

Although Jesus redeemed your spirit man, your body has not yet been redeemed. After Jesus rose from the dead, He promised that He would return to redeem your body.

> *But Christ has indeed been raised from the dead, the firstfruits of those who have fallen asleep. For since death came through a man, the resurrection of the dead comes also through a man.... We will not all sleep, but we will all be changed "in a flash, in the twinkling of an eye, at the last trumpet. For the trumpet will sound, the dead will be raised imperishable, and we will be changed"* (1 Corinthians 15:20-21,51b-52).

(Excerpts from *Releasing Your Potential*)

Wisdom Reflections

GOD intended your body to live forever. The ability of your finger to heal after you burn it, or of an incision to heal following surgery, attests to the small amount of eternal potential left in your body. God still intends that you will have an eternal body. He has promised that He will give life to your body at the resurrection of the dead. Your resurrected body will be like Adam's body before he sinned and Jesus' body after He rose from the dead. You will be able to touch your new physical body: *"Look at My hands and My feet. It is I Myself! Touch Me and see; a ghost does not have flesh and bones, as you see I have"* (Luke 24:39), and you will be able to eat: *"They gave Him a piece of boiled fish, and He took it and ate it in their presence"* (Luke 24:42-43).

In this life, your body is a hindrance. It gets tired, sick, bruised, and discouraged. As it grows older, you have to keep patching it together. That's why our society is so eager to find a fountain of youth. We don't like our aging bodies. We want them to be young again.

I like what Paul says in his second letter to the Corinthians: *"Therefore we do not lose heart. Though outwardly we are wasting away, yet inwardly we are being renewed day by day"* (2 Cor. 4:16).

God's making you a new home that will far exceed anything that plastic surgery can do for you. All plastic surgeons can do is patch your old body. God's in the business of giving you a new body. So don't worry if this body isn't all you'd like it to be. Patch it, fix it, do whatever you can to spruce it up. But don't equate your life with your body. God's going to get out of you all that He put in you. He wants you to start releasing your potential with the body you now have and to continue using your eternal capabilities long after this body has decayed. You are much more than your imperfect, deteriorating body.

Points to Ponder

Jesus promised that He would return to redeem your body.

God intended your body to live forever.

God's making you a new home.

God's in the business of giving you a new body.

Don't worry if your body isn't all you'd like it to be.

You are much more than your imperfect, deteriorating body.

Words of Wisdom

Modern Christians, especially those in the Western world, have generally been found wanting in the area of holiness of body. Gluttony and laziness, for example, were regarded by earlier Christians as sin. Today we may look on these as weaknesses of the will but certainly not sin. We even joke about our overeating and other indulgences instead of crying out to God in confession and repentance.

—Jerry Bridges, *The Pursuit of Holiness*[1]

For we were all baptized by one Spirit into one body—whether Jews or Greeks, slave or free—and we were all given the one Spirit to drink (1 Corinthians 12:13).

They that would keep themselves pure must have their bodies in subjection, and that may require, in some cases, a holy violence.

—Thomas Boston

Just as God the Father prepared a body for His Son to work through while He was on earth, so now the Son is preparing a Body for the Holy Spirit to flow through with His gifts. ...The secret to releasing that anointing is to learn how to yield not only your spirit and soul to Him, but also your body.

—Flo Ellers, *Activating the Angelic*[2]

MY WISDOM KEYS

_____

_____

_____

_____

_____

_____

_____

_____

_____

_____

_____

_____

_____

_____

32

Wisdom Over Fear and Anxiety

So overwhelmed is our world by the forces of evil that the love and peace God intended mankind to know have been replaced by hatred, jealousy, immorality, and anger. The pain of broken marriages and families has touched us all. The fear and anxiety that make us see even our own flesh and blood as enemies shadow our lives. The consequences of sexual promiscuity stare us in the face. Our environment is out of control and we are powerless to restrain it.

(Excerpts from *Releasing Your Potential*)

Wisdom Reflections

JESUS told a story that points to the solution of our messed up environment: A father had two sons. One day not long after he had asked his father for his share of the inheritance, the younger son left home and went to a distant country where he wasted his wealth in wild living. After he had spent everything, he became so hungry that he longed to eat the pigs' food.

> *When he came to his senses, he said, "How many of my father's hired men have food to spare, and here I am starving to death! I will set out and go back to my father and say to him: Father, I have sinned against heaven and against you. I am no longer worthy to be called your son; make me like one of your hired men." So he got up and went to his father* (Luke 15:17-20a).

What a telling phrase: "When he came to his senses." It reveals both the son's awareness of his poverty and his belief that his need could be met. He trusted his father's goodness enough to return and ask for forgiveness.

God is well acquainted with the insanity of your world. He offers Himself as the solution to your problems. Through Jesus, He has taken the initiative to restore the garden atmosphere with its gift of His presence, His fellowship, and the freedom to obey Him. But He will not force you to accept the new environment that He offers. Like the father of the wayward son, He waits for you to come to your senses and admit your sin and your need of His forgiveness. Only then can He make sense of your world.

God dealt with the problem of a polluted environment in Abram's life by asking him to leave everything (see Gen. 12:1-4a). Why? Because God knew that Abram's relationship with Him would be compromised by the negative influence of his family and friends.

Take a few moments now to examine your environment. Is it uplifting or degrading? Does it enrich your spiritual life or detract from the work of God's Spirit in your heart? Is obedience to God the norm for those with whom you spend your days, or do rebellion and disobedience characterize the lifestyles of your closest friends?

Moses instructed the Israelites to immerse themselves in God's commandments.

Points to Ponder

Fear and anxiety shadow our lives.

God is well acquainted with the insanity of your world.

God offers Himself as the solution to your problems.

God will not force you to accept the
new environment He offers.

God waits for you to come to your senses
and admit your sin and your need of His forgiveness.

Are you immersing yourself in God's commandments?

Words of Wisdom

After this, the word of the Lord came to Abram in a vision: "Do not be afraid, Abram. I am your shield, your very great reward" (Genesis 15:1).

◯

Our yesterdays present irreparable things to us; it is true that we have lost opportunities which will never return, but God can transform this destructive anxiety into a constructive thoughtfulness for the future. Let the past sleep, but let it sleep on the bosom of Christ. Leave the Irreparable Past in His hands, and step out into the Irresistible Future with Him.

—Oswald Chambers

◯

The beginning of anxiety is the end of faith, and the beginning of true faith is the end of anxiety.

—George Muller, "Signs of the Times" [1]

◯

The fear of the unknown can be crippling and is many times propagated by the skeptics who hope to confine us to the boundaries of their own limited understanding and attempt to present a possible interruption in their fragile world by a discovery of something greater than they can explain.

—Kim Clement, *Call Me Crazy, But I'm Hearing God* [2]

MY WISDOM KEYS

33

Wisdom of Marriage

One misconception many people have, both inside and outside the Church, is that the primary purpose of marriage is the propagation of the human race. The Bible indicates otherwise. Although in Genesis 1:28 God issued the charge to man to *"be fruitful and multiply,"* and although He defined marriage as the parameters in which reproduction should take place, procreation is not the primary purpose of marriage.

(Excerpts from *The Purpose and Power of Love and Marriage*)

Wisdom Reflections

OD'S command had to do with creation and subduing the created order.

God blessed them and said to them, "Be fruitful and increase in number; fill the earth and subdue it. Rule over the fish of the sea and the birds of the air and over every living creature that moves on the ground" (Genesis 1:28).

God created man—male and female—and He expected them to procreate and fill the earth with other humans, all of whom would rule over the created order as His vice-regents. Marriage was essentially a companionship covenant, the relational structure through which men and women—husbands and wives—would join and become one flesh and together rule the earthly dominion God had given them. Procreation is a function of marriage, but it is not the main focus.

As contemporary society plainly shows, marriage is not necessary for procreation. Unmarried men and women have no trouble at all making babies. In many parts of the world the number of out-of-wedlock births exceeds the number of babies born to married women. That is one reason why many scientists and sociologists are concerned that at the current rate, within one or two generations the global population will grow beyond the earth's capacity to sustain it.

Contrary to the common idea that marriage is mainly about making babies, marriage actually serves as a deterrent to rampant reproduction. There are at least two reasons for this. First, the social and moral requirement of being married before having children is still very strong in many, many places. Most people are still sensitive to the respectability of marriage, and that respect holds back a lot of procreation that would otherwise take place. Were it not for the institution of marriage, human beings would be even more prolific than they already are. Second, married couples who take their responsibilities seriously are careful not to conceive and give birth to more children than they can adequately love and care for. Paul had some strong words on this subject. *"If anyone does not provide for his relatives, and especially for his immediate family, he has denied the faith and is worse than an unbeliever"* (1 Tim. 5:8).

There is nothing sinful or unbiblical about careful advance family planning. (Let me make it clear that abortion is not "family planning," nor is it "health care." Abortion is the termination of life and the premeditated destruction of potential. It is the death of destiny and the interference of divine protocol. Abortion is rebellion against the known will of God.) On the contrary, true family planning is mature, responsible stewardship.

Points to Ponder

Marriage is a companionship covenant.

Procreation is a function of marriage,
but it is not the main focus.

The social and moral requirement of being married before
having children is still very strong in many, many places.

Most people are still sensitive to
the respectability of marriage.

Married couples who take their responsibilities seriously
are careful not to conceive and give birth to more children
than they can adequately love and care for.

True family planning is mature, responsible stewardship.

Words of Wisdom

Submit to one another out of reverence for Christ. Wives, submit to your husbands as to the Lord. For the husband is the head of the wife as Christ is the head of the church, His body, of which He is the Savior....Husbands, love your wives, just as Christ loved the church and gave Himself up for her...."For this reason a man will leave his father and mother and be united to his wife, and the two will become one flesh." This is a profound mystery—but I am talking about Christ and the church (Ephesians 5:21-23,25,31-32).

Marriage has all kinds of purposes: it provides the environment in which children may be born and properly reared. It provides the context in which the sexual instincts can be exercised in a God-intended way. But first and foremost, Genesis teaches us, it provides a very special friendship. In marriage a man and a woman can become the best of friends, knowing each other to such a depth that only God knows them better! This, too, is a gift from the Creator.

—Sinclair Ferguson, *A Heart for God*[1]

I am asking you to re-think the foundation of your marriage relationship. Let's be honest here. How many of us, when we first saw our mate-to-be, thought to ourselves, *Wow, now there is a girl/guy who would make me more effective in God's Kingdom?*

—Carl Hampsch, *Opposites Attract*[2]

For two people in a marriage to live together day after day is unquestionably the one miracle the Vatican has overlooked.

—Bill Cosby

Y WISDOM
KEYS

34

Wisdom and Baggage

Marriage is never just the coming together of two people, but a collision of their histories. It is a clash of cultures, experiences, memories, and habits. Marriage is the beautiful accommodation of another lifetime.

(Excerpts from *The Purpose and Power of Love and Marriage*)

Wisdom Reflections

BUILDING a strong marriage takes time, patience, and hard work. One of the hardest adjustments anyone faces is moving from single life to married life. Let's be honest: people do not change overnight. When you marry someone, you marry more than just a person; you "marry" an entire family, a complete history of experiences. That's why it is often so hard at first to understand this person who is now sharing your house and your bed. Both of you bring into your marriage 20 or 30 years of life experiences that color how you see and respond to the world. Most of the time you quickly discover that you see many things quite differently from each other. Difference of viewpoint is one of the biggest sources of stress and conflict in young marriages. Adjusting to these differences is critical to marital survival. Unfortunately, many marriages fail on precisely this point.

All of us filter what we see and hear through the lens of our own experiences. Personal tragedy, physical or sexual abuse, quality of family life when growing up, educational level, faith or lack of faith—any of these affect the way we view the world around us. They help shape our expectations of life and influence how we interpret what other people say or do to us.

None of us enter marriage "clean." To one degree or another, we each bring our own emotional, psychological, and spiritual baggage. Whatever our spouse says, we hear through the filter of our own history and experience. Our spouse hears everything we say the same way. Understanding and adjusting to this requires a lot of time and patience.

Over time and under the pressures of daily life, a husband and wife come to understand each other more and more. They begin to think alike, act alike, and even feel alike. They learn to sense each other's moods and often recognize what is wrong without even asking. Gradually, their personal attitudes and viewpoints shift and move toward each other so that their mentality is no longer "yours" and "mine," but "ours." This is when the gem-like quality of marriage shines most brilliantly. Fusion creates oneness.

Points to Ponder

Marriage is the beautiful accommodation
of another lifetime.

Building a strong marriage takes time,
patience, and hard work.

Difference of viewpoint is one of the biggest sources
of stress and conflict in young marriages.

Adjusting to these differences is critical to marital survival.

No one enters marriage "clean."

Fusion creates oneness.

Words of Wisdom

When a man is trying to win the heart of a woman, he studies her. He learns her likes, dislikes, habits, and hobbies. But after he wins her heart and marries, her, he often stops learning about her. The mystery and challenge of knowing her seems less intriguing, and he finds his interests drifting to other areas.

—Stephen and Alex Kendrick, *The Love Dare*[1]

Shhh. My husband's bothersome habits so annoyed me at times, I actually withheld love. Then he'd focus on my shortcomings and faults and shut me out. Ouch-Chihauhua. Although we lived in the same home, slept in the same bed, we lived in the Great Divide.

—*Reflections From the Powder Room on The Love Dare*[2]

What counts in making a happy marriage is not so much how compatible you are, but how you deal with incompatibility.

—Tolstoy

In marriage do thou be wise: prefer the person before money, virtue before beauty, the mind before the body; then thou hast a wife, a friend, a companion, a second self.

—William Penn

Y WISDOM
KEYS

35

Wisdom in Intimacy

The husband/wife relationship is the oldest and most pre-eminent of all human relationships. It predates and goes ahead of any other relationship, including parent/child, mother/daughter, father/son, and sister/brother. No relationship should be closer, more personal, or more intimate than that which exists between a husband and wife. Such intimacy involves not only love, but also knowledge. A husband and wife should know each other better than they know anyone else in the world. They should know each other's likes and dislikes, their quirks and pet peeves, their strengths and weaknesses, their good and bad qualities, their gifts and talents, their prejudices and blind spots, their graces and their character flaws. In short, a husband and wife should know everything about each other, even those undesirable traits that they hide from everyone else.

(Excerpts from *The Purpose and Power of Love and Marriage*)

Wisdom Reflections

THIS kind of knowledge is not automatic. It does not happen simply because two people get married. Relationship does not guarantee knowledge. One of the greatest problems in marriage or any other human relationship involves the labels we use. Words like "husband" and "wife," "mother" and "daughter," "sister" and "brother," or "father" and "son" describe various relational connections within a family. They also imply a knowledge or intimacy that may or may not exist.

For example, a mother and daughter may assume that they really know each other simply because their "labels" imply a close relationship. Certainly a mother knows her daughter and a daughter, her mother. This is not necessarily so. The same thing could be said of other relational connections. If I call you my brother or my sister I am implying that I already know you. I assume that because we are related there is no need for us to spend time together getting to know each other.

Labels that imply closeness and intimate knowledge may in reality hinder true relationship building. A husband and wife may assume that they know each other simply because they are married. As a result, they may do nothing more than scratch the surface, never plumbing the depths of each other's personalities to gain true knowledge and build a deep and intimate relationship.

Marriage is a lifelong journey into intimacy, but also into friendship. A husband and wife should be each other's best friend. There is no higher relationship. After all, who knows us better than our friends? Most of us will share with our friends things about ourselves that we never even tell our own families. Husbands and wives should have no secrets from each other. As their relationship develops they should grow into true friends, who know everything there is to know about each other, good and bad, and yet who love and accept each other anyway.

Points to Ponder

A husband and wife should know each other better than they know anyone else in the world.

A husband and wife should know everything about each other, even those undesirable traits that they hide from everyone else.

Relationship does not guarantee knowledge.

Labels that imply closeness and intimate knowledge may in reality hinder true relationship building.

Marriage is a lifelong journey into intimacy, but also into friendship.

As your relationship develops, you should grow into true friends and love and accept each other.

Words of Wisdom

Only by acceptance of the past, can you alter it.

—T.S. Eliot

That was the American dream, right? Grow up, marry, and have kids. However, many baby boomers of the 1960s became members of the me generation. They became more focused on their own needs rather than on the needs of others. Many times their wants also became their needs. The marriages of many baby boomers consisted of two people living together who were willing to receive 100 percent in exchange for giving little or nothing. Spouses in such unions became leeches joined together in a feeding frenzy designed to suck the life from each other.

—Doug Stringer, *Hope for a Fatherless Generation*[1]

Cold words freeze people, and hot words scorch them, and bitter words make them bitter, and wrathful words make them wrathful. Kind words also produce their image on men's souls; and a beautiful image it is. They smooth, and quiet, and comfort the hearer.

—Blaise Pascal

Affection is responsible for nine-tenths of whatever solid and durable happiness there is in our lives.

—C.S. Lewis

MY WISDOM KEYS

_____

_____

_____

_____

_____

_____

_____

_____

_____

_____

_____

_____

_____

36

Wisdom of Not Settling

I believe it is our Creator's will and desire that we decide to commit and dedicate ourselves, and determine within ourselves, to achieve the full maximization of our potential. Once again the questions are echoed: Have we fully utilized our abilities, talents, and gifts? Have we settled for the norm? Have we done our best? Have we allowed others to place limitations on our potential, or have we created self-imposed limitations?

(Excerpts from *Maximizing Your Potential*)

Wisdom Reflections

I T is essential that you come to grips with these questions because they are related to your personal fulfillment and your contribution to the human family and to the pleasure of your Creator. You have been endowed by your Creator with immeasurable treasures of ability specifically designed and tailored to accomplish everything your God-given purpose demands. You are equipped with all you need in order to do all you were created to do. However, the releasing of your potential is not up to God, but you. You determine the degree to which your destiny is accomplished. You determine the measure of your own success, success that is established by the Creator's assignment for your life.

Let me illustrate this with a personal experience. A few years ago I was privileged to purchase a name-brand video player/recorder for my family. As I arrived home with my purchase, I eagerly anticipated the exciting process of installing this wonder of technology. My children joined me as I sat on the floor of our living room to open this new treasure for our home. With unrestricted haste, I ripped open the carton and dislodged the machine from its Styrofoam packing, ignoring the manual booklet that fell to the floor beside me. Then, using the basic knowledge I had obtained from others whom I had observed installing similar machines, I proceeded to show my skill and wisdom. After connecting a few wires and turning a few switches, I was ready to test my expertise. I took a videocassette, placed it in the machine, turned on the television, and bingo—play. As the picture appeared on the screen, I felt a sense of pride and personal accomplishment. Turning to my son and daughter, I said, "There it is; we're in business."

We sat and watched for a while; then something occurred that changed my life forever. The inquisitive nature of my son began to work. He drew closer to the video machine, pointed to the row of 12 buttons, and asked, "What are they for, Dad?" In my attempt to show my fatherly wisdom and adult advantage in knowledge, I leaned forward and examined the buttons. I quickly realized that I was unable to explain any of the functions indicated by the buttons except those of pause, rewind, stop, and play, and I found myself exposing my ignorance to my young children.

I learned a lesson that day that would become a major pillar in my life.

Points to Ponder

Have you fully utilized your abilities, talents, and gifts?

Have you settled for the norm?

Have you done your best?

Have you allowed others to place limitations
on your potential?

Have you created self-imposed limitations?

You determine the degree to which your destiny
is accomplished.

Words of Wisdom

The use of means ought not to lessen our faith in God, and our faith in God ought not to hinder our using whatever means He has given us for the accomplishment of His own purposes.

—Hudson Taylor

Only by faith can we know God, receive Christ, live the Christian life, and take hold of His full provision for our needs. If you are going to live in the same powerful dimension of prayer Christ demonstrated, you must live your life and pray in faith!

—Morris Cerullo, *How to Pray*[1]

In the natural, if you quite a "cast-iron" court case halfway through the hearing, you would lose the case because you did not persist to the end. The devil knows how to use every delaying tactic to discourage us and try to stave off the inevitable. Therefore, we have to stay in there, even if there is delay, because God has to do everything righteously.

—Alan Vincent, *The Good Fight of Faith*[2]

Therefore, since we are surrounded by such a great cloud of witnesses, let us throw off everything that hinders and the sin that so easily entangles, and let us run with perseverance the race marked out for us (Hebrews 12:1).

MY WISDOM KEYS

_____

_____

_____

_____

_____

_____

_____

_____

_____

_____

_____

_____

_____

37

Wisdom of Not Being Normal

In reality, this experience [setting up the VCR] perfectly describes the lives of most of the nearly six billion people on planet Earth. Many live on only four functions: play, stop, pause, and rewind. Day after day they go to jobs they hate, stop to rest in homes they despise, pause long enough to vent their frustration, and then play the games people play pretending to be happy.

(Excerpts from *Maximizing Your Potential*)

Wisdom Reflections

WHAT a tragedy! They never experience the joy of the other functions of their lives, such as developing and refining their skills, fulfilling their God-given destiny, capturing their purpose for life, making long-range plans, expanding their knowledge base, increasing their exposure through travel, and exploring the limits of their gifts, talents, and abilities. They have chosen to accept the fate of the millions who have resigned themselves to a normal life, with normal activities, in the company of normal people, striving for normal goals, at a normal pace, with normal motivation, with a normal education, taught by normal teachers, who give normal grades, and live in normal homes, with normal families, leaving a normal heritage, for their normal children, who bury them in a normal grave. What a normal tragedy.

I am convinced that our Creator never intended for us to be normal—that is, to get lost in the crowd of "the norm." This is evidenced by the fact that among the 5.8 billion people on this planet, no two individuals are alike; their fingerprints, genetic code, and chromosome combinations are all distinct and unique. In reality, God created all people to be originals, but we continue to become copies of others. Too often we are so preoccupied with trying to fit in, that we never stand out.

You were designed to be distinctive, special, irreplaceable, and unique, so refuse to be "normal"! Go beyond average! Do not strive to be accepted, rather strive to be yourself. Shun the minimum; pursue the maximum. Utilize all your functions—maximize yourself! Use yourself up for the glory of your Creator. I admonish you: Die empty. Die fulfilled by dying unfilled.

This book is written for the "normal" person who wishes to exceed the norm. It is for the "ordinary" individual who has determined to be "extra-ordinary." It is for the individual just like you who knows that somewhere deep inside, there is still so much you have not released: so much yet to do, so much left to expose, so much to maximize.

Live life with all your might; give it all you have. Do it until there is nothing left to do because you have become all you were created to be, done all you were designed to do, and given all you were sent to give. Be satisfied with nothing less than your best.

Points to Ponder

Have you resigned yourself to a normal life?

Your Creator never intended you to be normal.

God created you as an original.

Are you so preoccupied with trying to fit in
that you never stand out?

You were designed to be distinctive,
special, irreplaceable, and unique.

Be satisfied with nothing less than your best.

Words of Wisdom

Therefore, I bind these lies and slanderous accusations to my person as an ornament; it belongs to my Christian profession to be vilified, slandered, reproached and reviled, and since all this is nothing but that, as God and my conscience testify, I rejoice in being reproached for Christ's sake.

—John Bunyan, *Grace Abounding*[1]

Whom He poured out on us generously through Jesus Christ our Savior, so that, having been justified by His grace, we might become heirs having the hope of eternal life (Titus 3:6-7).

Let no one imagine that he will lose anything of human dignity by this voluntary sell-out of his all to his God. He does not by this degrade himself as a man; rather he finds his right place of high honor as one made in the image of his Creator. His deep disgrace lay in his moral derangement, his unnatural usurpation of the place of God. His honor will be proved by restoring again that stolen throne. In exalting God over all, he finds his own highest honor upheld.

—A.W. Tozer

Two roads diverged in a wood, and I
I took the one less traveled by,
And that has made all the difference.

—Robert Frost

MY WISDOM KEYS

_____

_____

_____

_____

_____

_____

_____

_____

_____

_____

_____

_____

_____

_____

_____

38

Wisdom of Living Beyond

It was four o'clock on a cold, wet, winter morning. The snow had turned to mush, the wind blew with a vengeance, and the entire day seemed destined to be a source of depression. The small town appeared to be drugged as farmers, storekeepers, and street sweepers dragged themselves to their places of business. Suddenly a young boy about 12 years of age skipped along as he clutched an old cello case. The smile and quick stride revealed his anxiety and anticipation of reaching his intended destination.

The little boy's name was Pablo Casals. His interest in and commitment to music at such an early age inspired even his teacher and proved to be the seed of destiny for one of the world's greatest cellists.

Pablo Casals, at age 85, continued to rise early and spend most of the day practicing his cello. When he was asked during an interview why he continued to practice five hours a day, Casals replied, "Because I think I'm getting better."

(Excerpt from *Maximizing Your Potential*)

Wisdom Reflections

GREAT minds and souls, knowing always that what they have done must never be confused with what they can yet do, never settle for great work. As a matter of fact, the concept of retirement is a great myth that traps the untapped potential buried in millions of talented, gifted, and valuable individuals. This Western concept has caused many great men and women to settle for the average and to succumb to the mediocrity of the socially accepted standards of success. Please note, however, that all individuals throughout history who have left their footprints in the sands of destiny were driven by a passion greater than the desire for personal comfort.

Pablo Casals reminds us of the monumental character of men and women such as Abraham, the biblical patriarch who at 70 years of age, childless and frustrated, married to a barren woman, and being, with his wife, beyond the biological age of conceiving a child, accepted the vision of a baby destined to change the world and believed it would come to pass. Abraham saw the fruit of his faith when he was 100 years old.

Retirement was never a concept in the minds of these world changers. As a matter of fact, the apostle Paul, while spending his final days in prison under house arrest by order of the government of Rome, refused to retire or succumb to the environmental restrictions of age, imprisonment, and threats. Instead, he spent the rest of his days writing beautiful, life-changing, historical documents that constitute three-quarters of the New Testament and form the basis of most of the doctrine of the Christian Church today.

Like Pablo Casals, the apostle Paul believed that no matter what he had done, accomplished, achieved, or experienced in the past, there was always so much more left within to develop, release, and express. They both believed that the enemy of better is best and the tomb of the extra-ordinary is the ordinary.

Paul's perception of life, and the responsibility of each of us to maximize life to its fullest potential, is expressed in his final letter to Timothy. To this favorite young student, he wrote:

For I am already being poured out like a drink offering, and the time has come for my departure. I have fought the good fight, I have finished the race, I have kept the faith (2 Timothy 4:6-7).

Points to Ponder

Great minds and souls never settle for great work.

All individuals throughout history who have left their
footprints in the sands of destiny were driven by
a passion greater than the desire for personal comfort.

Retirement is a great myth that traps untapped potential.

Retirement is never a concept in the minds
of world changers.

The enemy of better is best, and the tomb of
the extra-ordinary is the ordinary.

Your responsibility is to maximize life to its fullest potential

Words of Wisdom

I have come that they may have life, and that they may have it more abundantly (John 10:10b NKJV).

God considers those who are of no account, those nobody expects to be anything; those whose family, friends, and relatives have thrown away and given up on. God takes those who are fearful and don't believe in themselves and makes them men and women of greatness with wealth, prestige, and honor—mighty men and women of valor!

—T.D. Jakes, *Power for Living*[1]

Excellence, the quality of being outstanding or superior, is often equated with winning a game or rising to the top of a profession. If encouraged to perform your work with excellence, you might think, "Hey, I'm not a professional athlete or the president of a company. I just do what I must to get by." You might even question whether what you do for a living really demands excellence. Do not buy into that kind of thinking, even for a moment. Regardless of your profession, God desires excellence from you.

—Kris Den Besten, *Shine: 5 Empowering Principles for a Rewarding Life*[2]

The badge of courage does not require that we walk through something dangerous. It simply requires that we continue to share God's love whenever and wherever we are.

—Tom White, *Voice of the Martyrs*[3]

Y WISDOM KEYS

39

Wisdom's Treasures

All the great things God has put inside us—our visions, dreams, plans, and talents—are satan's targets. He is afraid of men and women who have faith in God's wisdom and power because they take their visions and translate them into action. They not only set goals, they make them happen.

(Excerpts from *Maximizing Your Potential*)

Wisdom Reflections

THE deceiver fears the treasure we possess. His destructive tactics and deceptive influences come into our lives to nullify and entrap all God has given to us. He isn't going to let us fulfill our potential without encountering resistance from him. Indeed, his attack is so severe that Paul advised Timothy to seek the help of the Holy Spirit to meet and overcome it:

> *Guard the good deposit that was entrusted to you—*
> *guard it with the help of the Holy Spirit who lives in us*
> (2 Timothy 1:14).

Have no fear! God has given us everything we need to safeguard our hidden wealth from the schemes and deceit of the evil one. We must be careful, however, not to rely on weapons of human strength and wisdom. We cannot whip the enemy by ourselves, *"for the foolishness of God is wiser than man's wisdom, and the weakness of God is stronger than man's strength"* (1 Cor. 1:25). Only as we are *"strong in the Lord and in His mighty power"* (Eph. 6:10) can we withstand satan's onslaught against us. The Holy Spirit, sent by Jesus when we receive Him as Savior, is our Helper.

> *For our struggle is not against flesh and blood, but*
> *against the rulers, against the authorities, against the*
> *powers of this dark world and against the spiritual*
> *forces of evil in the heavenly realms. Therefore put on*
> *the full armor of God, so that when the day of evil*

comes, you may be able to stand your ground, and after you have done everything, to stand. Stand firm then, with the belt of truth buckled around your waist, with the breastplate of righteousness in place, and with your feet fitted with the readiness that comes from the gospel of peace. In addition to all this, take up the shield of faith, with which you can extinguish all the flaming arrows of the evil one. Take the helmet of salvation and the sword of the Spirit, which is the word of God. And pray in the Spirit on all occasions with all kinds of prayers and requests. With this in mind, be alert... (Ephesians 6:12-18).

This description of the armor of God details a plan to guard and protect your life against satan's invasion. You must understand the provisions of this plan and put them into practice if you want to defend your potential.

Points to Ponder

All the great things God has put inside you—your visions, dreams, plans, and talents—are satan's targets.

He is afraid of people like you who have faith in God's wisdom and power.

The deceiver fears the treasure you possess.

Only as you are *"strong in the Lord and in His mighty power"* (Eph. 6:10) can you withstand satan's onslaught against you.

The Holy Spirit, sent by Jesus when you received Him as Savior, is your Helper.

Understand the provisions of God's plan and put them into practice to defend your potential.

Words of Wisdom

Since the children have flesh and blood, He too shared in their humanity so that by His death He might destroy him who holds the power of death—that is, the devil (Hebrews 2:20).

⟍⟋

Satan, like a fisher, baits his hook according to the appetite of the fish.

—Thomas Adams, *A Puritan Golden Treasury*[1]

⟍⟋

When you renounce and return, the very act of turning your back on the evils and failures of the past while turning your heart and face toward God engages the ancient promises.... By renouncing everything that is not like God, you free yourself to embrace everything, everyone, and everything that is like God. In fact, it is your destiny!

—Donald Hilliard, *After the Fall*[2]

⟍⟋

He who does what is sinful is of the devil, because the devil has been sinning from the beginning. The reason the Son of God appeared was to destroy the devil's work (1 John 3:8).

MY WISDOM KEYS

_____

_____

_____

_____

_____

_____

_____

_____

_____

_____

_____

_____

40

Wisdom to Become

I admonish you, decide today to act on the rest of your sleeping dream. Commit yourself to the goal of dying empty. Jesus Christ our Lord, at the end of His earthly assignment, gave evidence of His success in maximizing His life by fulfilling all God's will for Him on earth. As He journeyed to the place of crucifixion, many people followed Him, mourning and wailing. Seeing them, Jesus said:

> *Daughters of Jerusalem, do not weep for Me; weep for yourselves and for your children* (Luke 23:28b).

The implication is evident: "I have completed My assignment, stayed through My course, and finished My task. I have emptied Myself of all My potential. Now it is your turn.".

(Excerpts from *Maximizing Your Potential*)

Wisdom Reflections

FIRST discover what you were born to be, then do it. Fulfill your own personal purpose for the glory of God. Your obedience to God's will and purpose for your life is a personal decision, but not a private one. God has designed the universe in such a way that the purposes of all mankind are interdependent; your purpose affects millions. Maximizing your potential is, therefore, necessary and critical. Your sphere of influence is much greater than your private world.

Suppose Mary had aborted Jesus, or Andrew had failed to introduce Peter to Jesus. What if Abraham had not left the Land of Ur, or Joseph had refused to go to Egypt. Or let's assume that Ananias had not prayed for Saul who became Paul, or that the little boy had refused to give Jesus his lunch. How different the biblical record might read! These examples show that although our obedience is always a personal decision, it is never a private matter.

Don't rob the next generation of your contribution to the destiny of mankind. Maximize yourself for God's glory. Remember, he who plants a tree plans for prosperity. *"The wise man saves for the future, but the foolish man spends whatever he gets"* (see Prov. 21:20).

Time is God's gift for accomplishing our purpose and fulfilling our potential. It begins the day we are born and ends when we die. The length of our physical life matches the days

244

required to fulfill our purpose because God planned for the maturing of our lives within the total days He has allotted to us. Therefore, we have sufficient time to maximize our potential. The question is, Will we waste or use wisely the days God has assigned to our lives?

The apostle Paul instructs us to *"see then that* [we] *walk circumspectly, not as fools but as wise, redeeming the time, because the days are evil"* (Eph. 5:15-16 NKJV). In other words, we must find our purpose and use our potential to accomplish it. Likewise, we need to consciously refuse to allow procrastination, discouragement, and the other enemies of our potential to induce us to waste even one day of our lives. Whenever we use our time to do things that neither release our potential nor help us progress toward the accomplishment of our purpose, we forfeit or delay the opportunity to reach the excellency and completion God intended for our lives.

The choice is yours. You are responsible to understand, release, and maximize your potential.

Points to Ponder

Commit yourself to the goal of dying empty.

Discover what you were born to be, then do it.

Fulfill your own personal purpose for the glory of God.

Don't rob the next generation of your contribution
to the destiny of mankind.

Time is God's gift for accomplishing your purpose
and fulfilling your potential.

Will you waste or use wisely the days God
has assigned to your life?

Words of Wisdom

So, ask God to give you the courage to say "no" to your own ways, doctrines, limitations, and fears. He will help you say "no" to the ways of this world and the things of the past, and He will make all things new in your life.

—Don Nori, *The Prayer God Loves to Answer*[1]

~

And God is able to make all grace abound to you, so that in all things at all times, having all that you need, you will abound in every good work (2 Corinthians 9:8).

~

Success is not the key to happiness. Happiness is the key to success. If you love what you are doing, you will be successful.

—Albert Schweitzer

~

Don't wait until everything is just right. It will never be perfect. There will always be challanges, obstacles and less than perfect conditions. So what. Get started now. With each step you take, you will grow stronger and stronger, more and more skilled, more and more self-confident and more and more successful.

—Mark Victor Hansen

~

Being confident of this, that He who began a good work in you will carry it on to completion until the day of Christ Jesus (Philippians 1:6).

MY WISDOM KEYS

_____

_____

_____

_____

_____

_____

_____

_____

_____

_____

_____

_____

_____

MY WISDOM KEYS

My Wisdom Keys

My Wisdom Keys

Endnotes

Note: Short quotes are taken from *Grace Quotes*: http://www.thegracetabernacle.org/quotes/grace_qs_bkgrnd.html and www.thinkexist.com (accessed September 16-21, 2009).

CHAPTER 1

1. Joseph W. Walker III, *Life Between Sundays* (Shippensburg, PA: Destiny Image Publishers, 2009), 37.

2. Elmer L. Towns, *Praying Paul's Letters* (Shippensburg, PA: Destiny Image Publishers, 2009), 56.

3. Jeff Jansen, *Glory Rising* (Shippensburg, PA: Destiny Image Publishers, 2009), 21.

CHAPTER 2

1. Don Nori Sr., *You Can Pray in Tongues* (Shippensburg, PA: Destiny Image Publishers, 2009), 55.

2. Joseph Mattera, *Kingdom Revolution* (Shippensburg, PA: Destiny Image Publishers, 2009), 137.

CHAPTER 3

1. Sid Roth, *There Must be Something More* (Shippensburg, PA: Destiny Image Publishers, 2009), 39.

2. John MacArthur, *The Book on Leadership* (Nashville, TN: Thomas Nelson, 2006), 51.

CHAPTER 4

1. Larry Kreider, *House to House* (Shippensburg, PA: Destiny Image Publishers, 2009), 193.

CHAPTER 5

1. Banning Leibscher, *Jesus Culture* (Shippensburg, PA: Destiny Image Publishers, 2009), 94.

CHAPTER 6

1. Elmer L. Towns, *Praying the Heart of David* (Shippensburg, PA: Destiny Image Publishers, 2009), 178.

2. Faisal Malick, *Positioned to Bless* (Shippensburg, PA: Destiny Image Publishers, 2008), 84-85.

CHAPTER 8

1. James Wilson, *Living as Ambassadors of Relationships* (Shippensburg, PA: Destiny Image Publishers, 2008), 161.

2. James W. Goll and Lou Engle, *The Call of the Elijah Revolution* (Shippensburg, PA: Destiny Image Publishers, 2008), 137-139.

3. *Ibid.*, 208.

CHAPTER 9

1. Noel Jones and Scott Chaplan, *Vow of Prosperity* (Shippensburg, PA: Destiny Image Publishers, 2007), 48.

2. Sinclair Ferguson, *A Heart for God* (1987, by permission Banner of Truth, Carlisle, PA), 31.

CHAPTER 10

1. Donald Whitney, *Spiritual Disciplines for the Christian Life* (1991, used by permission of NavPress), 127. See http://www. thegracetabernacle.org/quotes/Service-Encouragement.htm (accessed September 18, 2009).

2. Bill Wilson, *Christianity in the Crosshairs* (Shippensburg, PA: Destiny Image Publishers, 2004), 28-29.

CHAPTER 11

1. Rick Warren, *The Purpose Driven Life* (Grand Rapids, MI: Zondervan, 2002), 22.

CHAPTER 12

1. Billy Joe Daugherty, *When Life Throws You a Curve* (Shippensburg, PA: Destiny Image Publishers, 2004), 87.

2. Don Nori, *The Prayer God Loves to Answer* (Shippensburg, PA: Destiny Image Publishers, 2006), 75.

CHAPTER 13

1. Dr. Heidi Baker, in *God's Supernatural Power,* Frank DeCenso Jr., ed. (Shippensburg, PA: Destiny Image Publishers, 2009), 53.

2. Bill Johnson, *Strengthen Yourself in the Lord* (Shippensburg, PA: Destiny Image Publishers, 2007), 52.

CHAPTER 14

1. Steve Shultz, *Can't You Talk Louder God?* (Shippensburg, PA: Destiny Image Publishers, 2007), 50.

CHAPTER 16

1. T.D. Jakes, *Release Your Anointing* (Shippensburg, PA: Destiny Image Publishers, 2008), 72.

2. John Crowder, *The New Mystics* (Shippensburg, PA: Destiny Image Publishers, 2006), 45.

3. Francis J. Sizer, *Into His Presence* (Shippensburg, PA: Destiny Image Publishers, 2007), 205-206.

CHAPTER 17

1. Leigh Valentine, *Successfully You!* (Shippensburg, PA: Destiny Image Publishers, 2008), 148.

2. Joyce Meyer, "Everyday Answers, Two are Better than One," *Joyce Meyer Ministries*; http://www.joycemeyer. org/OurMinistries/EverydayAnswers/Articles/art6. htm?&MSHiC=65001&L=10&W=IDEAL%20IDEAS%20 idea%20&Pre=%3CFONT%20STYLE%3D%22color%3A%20 %23000000%3B%20background-color%3A%20 %23FFFF00%22%3E&Post=%3C/FONT%3E (accessed September 19, 2009).

CHAPTER 18

1. Millicent Hunter, *Don't Die in the Winter* (Shippensburg, PA: Destiny Image Publishers, 1995), 61.

2. Don Nori Sr., *Manifest Presence* (Shippensburg, PA: Destiny Image Publishers, 1988, 2009), 62.

3. John Milton, *Paradise Lost* (Shippensburg, PA: Destiny Image Publishers, 2007), 62.

Chapter 19

1. Henry Virkler, *Hermeneutics* (Ada, MI: Baker Books, 1981), 219.

2. C.S. Lewis, *Mere Christianity,* http"//www.philiosophyforlife.com/mc21.htm.

Chapter 20

1. Elmer L. Towns, *Praying the Gospels* (Shippensburg, PA: Destiny Image Publishers, 2007), 128.

Chapter 21

1. Gene Getz, *Elders and Leaders* (Chicago: Moody Press, 2003), 267.

Chapter 22

1. Lynn Hiles, *The Revelation of Jesus Christ* (Shippensburg, PA: Destiny Image Publishers, 2007), 98.

2. Alistair Begg, *Made For His Pleasure* (Chicago: Moody Press, 1996), 39.

3. Richard Booker, *Living in His Presence* (Shippensburg, PA: Destiny Image Publishers, 2007), 27.

Chapter 23

1. Noel Jones, *God's Gonna Make You Laugh* (Shippensburg, PA: Destiny Image Publishers, 2007), 94.

2. John H. Gerstner, *Theology for Everyman* (Chicago: Moody Press, 1965), Chapter 4.

CHAPTER 24

1. Cal Thomas, "The Authority of the State," *Tabletalk,* March 2009. Used by Permission.

2. Robert Stearns, *Prepare the Way (or Get Out of the Way!)* (Shippensburg, PA: Destiny Image Publishers, 1999), 206.

3. Mark Dever, *Nine Marks of a Healthy Church* (Wheaton, IL: Crossway Books, 2000), 214.

CHAPTER 25

1. R.C. Sproul, "Statism," *Tabletalk,* September 2008. Used by Permission.

2. Israel Kim, *Find Your Promised Land* (Shippensburg, PA: Destiny Image Publishers, 2009), 95.

CHAPTER 26

1. Bruce Allen, *Promise of the Third Day* (Shippensburg, PA: Destiny Image Publishers, 2007), 119.

2. John Piper, "Desiring God," copyright Bethlehem Baptist Church, 1996, page 56. Used by permission.

CHAPTER 27

1. T.D. Jakes, *Can You Stand to be Blessed?* (Shippensburg, PA: Destiny Image Publishers, 1994), 11.

2. Derek Prince, *Faith to Live By* (New Kensington, PA: Whitaker House, 1977), 162.

Chapter 28

1. Don Nori Sr., *The Love Shack* (Shippensburg, PA: Destiny Image Publishers, 2009), 52-53.

2. Keith Hudson, *The Cry* (Shippensburg, PA: Destiny Image Publishers, 2009), 93.

Chapter 29

1. Kris Vallotton, *Sexual Revolution* (Shippensburg, PA: Destiny Image Publishers, 2008), 160-161.

2. www.abortionno.org (accessed September 20, 2009).

Chapter 30

1. A.W. Pink, *The Attributes of God* (Ada, MI: Baker Book House), 49.

2. Greg Holmes, *If He Builds It, They Will Come* (Shippensburg, PA: Destiny Image Publishers, 2007), 140-141.

3. Scott Hafemann, *The God of Promise and the Life of Faith* (Wheaton, IL: Crossway Books, 2001), 203.

Chapter 31

1. Jerry Bridges, *The Pursuit of Holiness* (Colorado Springs, CO: NavPress © 1996), 108. Used by permission of NavPress. All rights reserved. www.thegracetabernacle.org (accessed September 20, 2009).

2. Flo Ellers, *Activating the Angelic* (Shippensburg, PA: Destiny Image Publishers, 2008), 60.

CHAPTER 32

1. George Muller, "Signs of the Times," *Christianity Today*, v. 35, n. 1.

2. Kim Clement, *Call Me Crazy, But I'm Hearing God* (Shippensburg, PA: Destiny Image Publishers, 2007), 101.

CHAPTER 33

1. Sinclair Ferguson, *A Heart for God* (1987, by permission Banner of Truth, Carlisle, PA), 32.

2. Carl Hampsch, *Opposites Attract* (Shippensburg, PA: Destiny Image Publishers, 2007), 79-80.

CHAPTER 34

1. Stephen and Alex Kendrick, *The Love Dare* (Nashville, TN: B&H Publishing Group, 2008), 86.

2. Shae Cooke, Tammy Fitzgerald, Donna Scuderi, and Angela Rickabaugh Shears, *Reflections from the Powder Room on The Love Dare* (Shippensburg, PA: Destiny Image Publishers, 2009), 89.

CHAPTER 35

1. Doug Stringer, *Hope for a Fatherless Generation* (Shippensburg, PA: Destiny Image Publishers, 2009), 50-51.

CHAPTER 36

1. Morris Cerullo, *How to Pray* (Shippensburg, PA: Destiny Image Publishers, 2004), 201.

2. Alan Vincent, *The Good Fight of Faith* (Shippensburg, PA: Destiny Image Publishers, 2008), 130.

Chapter 37

1. John Bunyan, *Grace Abounding* (Darlington, England: Evangelical Press, 2000), 143.

Chapter 38

1. T.D. Jakes, *Power for Living* (Shippensburg, PA: Destiny Image Publishers, 2009), 108.

2. Kris Den Besten, *Shine: 5 Empowering Principles for a Rewarding Life* (Shippensburg, PA: Destiny Image Publishers, 2008), 89.

Chapter 39

1. Thomas Adams, in *A Puritan Golden Treasury* (compiled by I.D.E. Thomas, by permission of Banner of Truth, Carlisle, PA, 2000), 290.

2. Donald Hilliard, *After the Fall* (Shippensburg, PA: Destiny Image Publishers, 2007), 109.

Chapter 40

1. Don Nori, *The Prayer God Loves to Answer* (Shippensburg, PA: Destiny Image Publishers, 2006), 77.

For Information on Bahamas Religious Tourism

Tel: 1-800-224-3681
Web site: worship.bahamas.com

MYLES MUNROE INTERNATIONAL
The Diplomat Center

P.O. Box N-9583
Nassau, Bahamas
Tel: 242-341-6423

Web site: www.mylesmunroeinternational.com
E-mail: mmi@mylesmunroeinternational.com